man
management
for women

Published by Cassell Illustrated
A Member of Octopus Publishing Group Ltd.
2-4 Heron Quays
London
E14 4JP

ISBN 1 84403 376 7
EAN 9781844033768

Conceived, designed and produced by
Quid Publishing Ltd
Level Four
Sheridan House
114 Western Road
Hove BN3 1DD
England
www.quidpublishing.com

Author: Jane Moseley
Additional research: Jackie Strachan
Design: rehabdesign
Illustrations: Matt Pagett

Printed and bound in China by Regent Publishing Services, Ltd

NOTE
The information in this book is not intended to replace the advice of a of a physician or medical practitioner. Always check with a health-care provider before beginning a new health program. The author, publisher and copyright holder assume no responsibility for any injury, loss or damage caused or sustained as a consequence of the use and application of the contents of this book.

man
management
for women

CONTENTS

Physical ID

Emotional ID

Love & Friendship

Ideal Man

Manscellany

Tools & Techniques

'If Only Men Were More Like Women (or, Better Still, Dogs and Cats)...'

Some women live with cats, others with dogs, a few with goldfish and many millions with men. Cats are cats, dogs are dogs, neither are humans (although often preferable to them), but, as with men, there are countless varieties. Some are equipped with long tails, hairy bodies and angular features, others are smoother, shorter of tail and rounder of face. Large numbers of feline and canine friends may be sitting devotedly at women's feet as they read this, perhaps due in part to the ever-increasing numbers of books on how to train, care for, understand, support and communicate with many-legged loved ones at their disposal. On the other hand, there are billions of men in the world but only a handful of books on how to really understand, appreciate and live in harmony with them.

Man Management for Women is aimed at all those women out there who have tried their hand at cat and dog whispering, have got those skills under their belt and want to become Man Whisperers. It is for all those females who want to learn how to see inside the male mind, to understand how it works, to communicate more easily and successfully with the male species.

Many women are sent out into the big wide world, equipped with a rather inadequate toolbox marked 'Men, How to Find, Identify and Deal Successfully with Them'. Hopefully, this book will fit neatly in that box of tricks and help build a bridge between the sexes. Its aim is to become an invaluable tool in the creation of increased understanding, appreciation, harmony and partnership between men and women. It's a big ask, but then bigger is sometimes better, and nothing is really too big for women, after all, is it?

Men and women are different – everybody knows that. Now it's time to realise in what ways and to what extent men differ from women and then deal with it. Men are from a different planet – yeah, yeah, so what's new? Somehow, they got their act together enough to sort out transport to this one (or perhaps the women did it for them), so let's get over it. Firstly, we need to do a physical ID and check out

PETER PERFECT

Understanding where your man is coming from will help you to manage your relationship more effectively

what sort of men are out there. Imagine a book called *Canine Management for Women*, in which there would be descriptions of bulldogs and chihuahuas, rotweilers and poodles, gentle fluffy pooches and fierce, snarling, bare-toothed hounds. Some would be blessed with athletic physiques and prize-winning natures. Others might have the former but not the latter, or vice versa, but often not both. It is the same with men.

Man Management for Women looks at the male species, its physical and emotional make-up, its body, its brain and its variety. Learn how to manage all aspects of your man, just like your dog or cat. He will soon be eating out of your hand.

Man Talk

Take a few minutes to think about your man and how you would describe him (to a girlfriend).
It will help to focus your mind on his good points (or not).

IF YOU HAD TO DESCRIBE YOUR MALE PARTNER WHICH OF THE FOLLOWING NOUNS WOULD SPRING TO MIND:

A) DREAM
B) NIGHTMARE
C) TORTURE
D) CHALLENGE
E) JOY

DESCRIBE THE LEARNING CURVE INVOLVED IN HANDLING YOUR MAN:

A) VERTICAL
B) GRADUAL
C) HORIZONTAL
D) OFF THE CHART
E) OFF THE PLANET

IF YOU WERE PUTTING YOUR MAN ON E-BAY HOW MUCH WOULD YOU EXPECT THE BID TO GO TO?

A) £50
B) £150
C) £1,000
D) £10,000
E) £1M

WHICH (IF ANY) OF THE FOLLOWING ADJECTIVES BEGINNING WITH 'UN-' WOULD YOU USE MOST WHEN TALKING TO HIM?

A) UNCOMMUNICATIVE
B) UNHELPFUL
C) UNSUPPORTIVE
D) UNSIGHTLY
E) UNTHINKING

HOW GREAT IS THE DIFFERENCE BETWEEN WOMEN AND MEN IN YOUR VIEW:

A) SLIGHT
B) HUGE
C) TOTAL
D) MINISCULE
E) COMPLETE, 100%

IF YOU HAD TO DESCRIBE YOUR STATUS AS A MANAGER OF MEN AT THIS STAGE, WOULD YOU SAY YOU WERE:

A) AN EXPERT
B) A LEARNER
C) A DUNCE
D) AN APPRENTICE
E) SEMI-RETIRED

![icon] Physical ID

The Body
Getting to know your man's body is not just about seeing him with only his boxer shorts on. It involves understanding which part does what and how to help if it gets into difficulty.

The Brain
This book will help you understand what is going on inside as well as outside. Run your fingers through his hair and explore the workings of his mind.

The Stomach
It is important to encourage him to eat properly in order to stay healthy. Otherwise, he may have to make more visits to the doctor and he won't like the idea of that.

'A man's body may be his temple, but not all women will have faith in it.'
CAROLINE FOSTER, 2005

Exercise
Enjoy a healthy lifestyle together. A combination of good diet and lots of exercise is good for both of you.

It's Time to Clock that Body

It's always polite to start any kind of relationship with a formal introduction. Parties just don't go with the same swing if people don't get to know each other. So let's do it: 'Woman, I'd like you to get to know Man.' That's what this book is all about, after all. 'Man meets Woman' is another ballgame entirely. OK, now that's over with, let's get physical, or 'physiqual', to be more precise. It's time to check out the bodywork and see which part does what. Once you are more acquainted with the machine you will feel more confident about handling it, or so the car salesman says. Get to know more about your man's physique and the physical will fall into place. It's like reading the instructions and looking at the diagrams before you turn on the machine.

Now meet the three basic body types. They all end in morph, meaning 'shape,' and you can use the following information to decide which morphman you are dealing with. Mesomorphs are naturally athletic and muscular, with narrow hips and a well-built upper torso; they are low on body fat, gain muscle easily and have a medium metabolism. In the alpha(male)bet of life, they are the letter 'V'. Ectomorphs, on the other hand, use all the 'L' words: long, lean and lanky. High on metabolic rate, low on fat, sometimes below average on the muscle front, long of limb and narrow of shoulder. They will call the letter 'I' to mind visually. Endomorphs, on the third hand, are rounded, stout and rather heavy set. They put on muscle quickly, but acquire fat with similar ease and aren't what you would call chiselled. They carry most of their body fat around the hip and stomach area. Their metabolism is slow. No letter of the alphabet reflects them properly, but if you cast a glance at the figure '8' on your calculator and expand the lower half, you've got his number. That does not mean he is not an alpha(bet)male, however. Read on.

As discussed, your guy will be one of these morphs, or perhaps even a mixture – an ectomeso or a mesoecto. If he is an ecto-endo, you are dating an alien. However, it is important to remember that your man (just like you) can't help being ecto, endo or meso (so don't laugh until you check out your own morph status in the mirror). With the right exercise and diet, he can stop becoming morphat (ouch!). Help him to get a handle on muscle rather than a grip on his own love handles.

What should your morph do? Mesomorphs, all muscle, should turn their hand to weight training, gymnastics, boxing, sprinting, martial arts or power-lifting – pretty much anything that requires sheer force. Ectomorphs, long and lanky, are great at running marathons, playing basketball, riding bikes and doing gym routines and aerobics (they would generally look better in leotards than women, irritatingly enough, but few of them can be persuaded to sport them). Endomorphs, on the third hand, should turn to swimming and walking, maybe doing a spot of aerobics, a few weights and a go on the rowing machine or treadmill, but they should beware of adding too much muscle, or they will become 88 (two fat ladies in bingo but not high on the score card of attractiveness).

PETER PERFECT

Helping your man get a grip on his physique may mean there will be less for you to get a hold of.

Questionnaire

It is important to eye up your man from time to time to check how he is looking. Catch glimpses of him clothed, semi-clothed or unclothed and tick some of the following boxes. Is he the answer? That is the question you really need to ask yourself.

YOU SEE HIM BARE-CHESTED. DOES HE HAVE:

A) PECS TO DIE FOR
B) A REJECT FROM A PIGEON
C) A CHEST SO HOLLOW YOU COULD LOSE YOUR HEAD IN IT
D) BIGGER BOOBS THAN YOU
E) A NICE SHAPELY CHEST

EXAMINE HIS BELLY NEXT TIME HE IS IN HIS BOXERS. IS IT:

A) A BEER BARREL
B) A TWO-PACK
C) A SIX-PACK
D) GUTTED
E) A BUY-ONE-GET-ONE-FREE OFFER

MOVING DOWN TO HIS CHEEKS, WHAT WORDS COME TO MIND:

A) BRAD
B) GRANDDAD
C) HOW SAD
D) THAT'S MY LAD!
E) THEY DRIVE ME MAD...

NOW TO HIS THIGHS... IF THEY WERE A PAIR OF NUTCRACKERS WHAT WOULD THEY CRACK?

A) A GRAPE
B) A MELON
C) A COCONUT
D) A MONKEY NUT
E) A PILATES BALL

THINK OF A LETTER OF THE ALPHABET THAT DESCRIBES THE OVERALL SHAPE OF YOUR MAN'S UPPER TORSO (THAT'S THE BIT ABOVE THE WAIST. SO RAISE YOUR GAZE, GIRLS):

A) V
B) U
C) X
D) I
E) O

NOW TO HIS LOWER HALF AND HIS THIGHS DOWN TO THE GROUND. WHICH NUMBER COMES TO MIND?

A) 11
B) 88
C) 99
D) 00
E) 22

1. If he is a V88, your man has nice broad shoulders, a tapered waist and good muscular legs.

2. If he is a U22, he has a beer belly that droops over his belt and spindly legs that set off in different directions due to a distinct lack of muscle.

3. A V11 has strong shoulders, a tight waist and spaghetti legs.

Get the picture? If your visual skills are letting you down, check out the Manscellany on page 100.

Let's Get Physical

As they say in the media, let's take it from the top. Let's eyeball an average guy, top to toe. It's a bit of an eyeful. Some bits are awesome and others more awful. However, it is important to be able to ID every part, or you may miss out on a whole lot of facts, fun or frolics. Got your pencil? Let's roll...

Top of Head

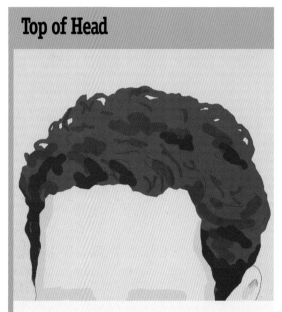

This is the thinking part of a man – the intellectual HQ. For more information about exactly what goes on inside here see page 48. It is important to understand the inner workings to stay in with half a chance of reading a guy's mind. Yes, his brain is probably bigger than yours but with all that thinking about sex and procreation, he needs all the cells he can get.

Men and women think differently in a number of areas, and these will be explored in greater detail later. Brains – male and female – are largely water-based. If he says his head is swimming, it may well be. Check he's not using beer as a lubricant for his thinking engine. And try to persuade him to change his hairstyle more than once every ten years.

Eyes

These are the windows onto his soul. Pay close attention – if the mouth is saying one thing, the eyes might be signalling something completely different. If he sports sunglasses day and night, he may well have something to hide. Remember, crying is acceptable – it shows your man is in touch with his emotions and confident enough in his manhood to show that emotion. Encourage him to express his sadness. If he cries like a baby at Bambi you may need to talk to him about it – tell him cry-babies are only attractive to their mothers. But let him know it's OK for big guys to cry when things get really serious. Tears are better out than in – unlike certain other bodily functions men indulge in rather more frequently than women...

Nose

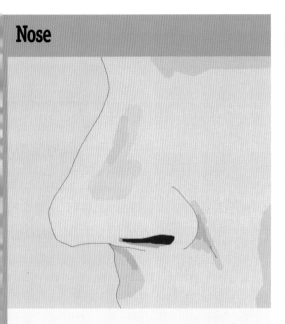

Best viewed in profile this feature may reveal much about your man (and remember, any children will have around a 50% chance of inheriting it). Aristocratic, aquiline and imposing indicates a strong, thoughtful, potentially arrogant man – you'll need to stand up to him. A button, snub nose can be sweet if a little submissive in appearance and may require you to treat him with more care. A ski-slope nose can mean a tendency to exaggerate, if not deliberately mislead, so keep an eye out for that (and don't let him poke you in it when you embrace).

After the age of about 30, his nasal hair may start to protrude. Buy him some decent nose-hair trimmers and ban the scissors – one slip equals big snip. (See page 72 for the importance of a sense of smell to your relationship.)

Mouth

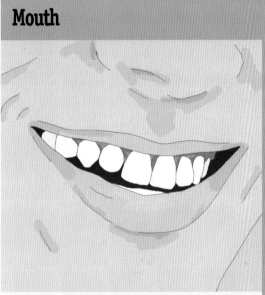

Now you're talking. This is the communication HQ – both verbal and non-verbal. He will use verbal communication to get what he wants, so keep an ear out for what he is really saying and why. Don't let him too close to your ear unless you are fully in control and can handle sweet nothings or garlic breath. On the hygiene front, leave articles around explaining the importance of flossing if he is unaware of it and take advantage of 2-for-1 offers on new toothbrushes to prevent him looking down in the mouth. Encourage him to give up smoking. Tell him licking out Popeye's pipe bowl would be more fun than kissing a smoker.

A strong, protruding jaw indicates higher levels of testosterone. If a man with a jutting jaw thrusts it forward in your presence, he is indicating his defiance.

Let's Get More Physical

Without getting too 'below the belt' about matters, you need to make sure that you check out the whole package when assessing a man. Put another way: to be on the safe side, you need to read the small print when you sign yourself up for a major new project. Eyes down, girls...

Skin

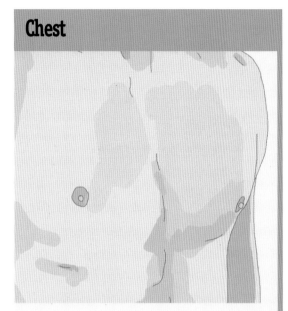

Encourage your man to protect his skin with a high factor sun cream and to exfoliate and moisturise regularly. Show him how you do it – devise a joint bathroom beauty routine. Convince him that skin care is not just for girls. Excessive exposure to sunlight can cause skin cancer. If your man has fair skin, he is at even greater risk and will need to be vigilant. Help him to do it.

It's up to you if you like facial hair. If you don't, try explaining gently that you like furniture in the home, not on your man's face. Tell him to concentrate on garden topiary rather than the facial variety; tell him his beard hides his handsome features or his moustache tickles when you kiss. After all, it is just another thing he has to wash and trim.

Chest

The chest is home to the vital organ – the heart. You need to understand how to manage this on a number of levels. On the nutritional front, he may well need your advice and support in order to ensure its healthy maintenance, avoiding damage from poor diet and alcohol intake. Keep his arteries as free-flowing as your channels of communication (for nutritional advice, see page 76). On the emotional front he may well need some guidance, too. Sometimes the brain sends messages further down the body without stopping at the heart, and messages are sent from below to the head in a vice versa kind of way. Try to intercept them at mouth and heart level and talk to him about how he feels – but pick your time (see page 42). Don't tackle him when he has retreated into defensive mode and is lurking in his emotional shed.

Belly

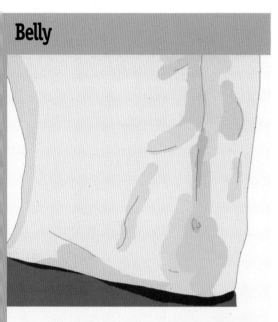

The T(owel) and B(utt) Zones

The belly houses the engine room of your man's body. If he fills it with the wrong type of fuel it won't work properly and may conk out sooner than either of you would like. Its pipes will clog up and end up going phutt. Encourage him to eat less junk food and go for healthy options instead – steer him towards low-fat meals, with lots of fish, chicken, fruit, veggies and nuts (instead of sweets and crisps) and fewer pints of beer on the side. Adopt a healthy-eating programme together so you can motivate and congratulate one another. Diet as a team or ask one of his mates to challenge him to a joint regime. He won't be able to resist a bet. Promise him a romantic weekend away if he loses those extra inches or kilos in a set time. Stick the results on the refrigerator door. Keep your promise, though. Don't pull out once he has reached goal. If you exercise together, you will be able to see more of each other while seeing less.

This is the hotbed of action (or the cool couch, depending on overall health, stamina, alcohol intake and emotional flagging). It is important for both of you to be aware that smoking and being overweight can impact negatively on fertility. Too much alcohol can also adversely affect proceedings in the romantic arena. Drinker's Droop is not a quaint country village where you go for a dirty weekend. The T-Zone may become No-Go Zone in both senses. For a firmer B-Zone, tell him to lie on his back on the floor (or in bed) and squeeze Mr and Mrs Gluteus Maximus together in a tight clinch while counting to five. Repeating 'I love you so very, very, very much' should help. Or 'Yes, I will do the vacuuming, dusting and ironing.' Lunges, squats and leg presses all help to develop the Gluteal Brothers (Maximus, Medius and Minimus). Remind him that a firm butt is not just physically attractive – without round, muscular buttocks we would still be walking around on all fours like our early ancestors.

Don't Let Him (Let Himself) Go

Bigger is not always better, and making less of yourself can have positive consequences. You may have to encourage your man to lower his sights and check out if he's expanding his physical horizons. And you can practise what you preach by joining him in eating healthily and exercising regularly, too. Obesity is a huge problem in today's world, and many people lead very sedentary, inactive lifestyles.

An average day can consist of a commute by bus, car or train (and not foot) to work, many hours spent seated, often with incorrect posture, in front of a computer, too much coffee, processed, ready-made food eaten in haste, a frustrating commute home and an evening spent watching television with a pre-packed or take-out meal, with more than the odd snack, cookie, beer, cocktail, wine or cigarette in between.

Try this maths conundrum on your man. When does five equal ten out of ten? Correct answer: when you eat five portions of fruit and veg a day. You get zero out of ten if you ignore the following No-No's.

Talking Tums

Motivate your man

Walking is great exercise. Try to work out exactly how much you do on a day-to-day basis. The total may come as a surprise – most people do much less than they think.

❌ No-No's

All the following activities could seriously damage your health:

1. Sofa, so bad

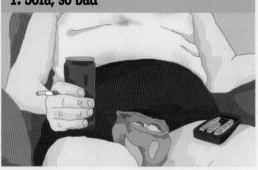

Don't let him become a sofa slob. The motto 'If you can't beat them, join them' doesn't work in this case. You will only end up as a couch chick yourself. It's fine to relax after a hard day and chill out for a while, but an entire evening spent glued to the television flexing finger muscles on the remote control is not good for either of you.

2. Carrot, not stick

Don't impose a rigid and dull regime or neither of you will stick to it. Talking of which, try the carrot and stick approach. After a long walk or a jogging session, offer to give him a massage – he can then return the favour. Don't make him associate exercise with pain. It can be lots of fun and a chance to spend more time together.

3. Positive, not negative

Don't make him feel you are trying to change him into a new person or he will become defensive and reluctant. If you suggest working to become both healthier and more energetic as a joint effort, rather than a personal crusade, he will see it as a challenge rather than a criticism. Think how you would feel if he bought you four diet books for Christmas.

4. Play doctors and nurses

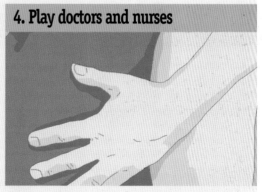

Don't forget that checking each other out physically can be fun. You could try playing doctors and nurses (with or without the uniforms). The feel good factor could be just that. Have a good feel of each other and check for lumps and bumps in the wrong places and then perhaps in the right ones. Enough said.

Take His Body into Your Hands

Depending on which model is in the garage, your involvement in the healthy maintenance of its bodywork and regularity of engine check-ups will vary. You may be dealing with a finely tuned machine and keen to monitor closely how much fuel is guzzled and what distance is covered at what average speed. Or, you may be sharing garage space with a slightly cranky machine that doesn't go very far or very fast and whose fuel gauge is off the scale. The exhaust pipe coughs and splutters, the brakes have gone and things are in reverse.

Some of you will be in the driver's or the passenger seat on the health front. Some guys take their health routine into their own hands but others need help. Lots of guys like going to the doctor or dentist as much as cleaning behind the refrigerator after doing a pile of ironing. Here are a few tips on how to keep an eye on their bodies. You don't want them to end up on the scrap heap.

Talking Bodies

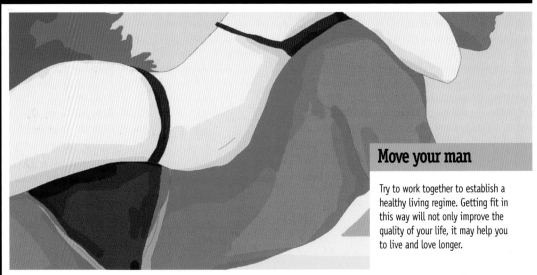

Move your man

Try to work together to establish a healthy living regime. Getting fit in this way will not only improve the quality of your life, it may help you to live and love longer.

Do-Do's

All the following activities could seriously improve your health:

1. Embrace exercise

If your man can't spell exercise never mind indulge in 30 minutes of it per day, try to encourage him by suggesting you do more activities together. Get a joint membership of a gym, go swimming, jogging or walking before or after work (a dog helps on that score and is rewarding on lots of other levels too, like stress relief) and motivate (bribe) him with the promise of a drink/hug/massage later.

2. Say 'wow'

Encourage your guy by congratulating him on how sexy you find him when he is all healthy, active and outdoorsy, how he looks good on the pitch or the court or in his sports gear. Exercise triggers all those happy hormones and can be great for a relationship. Sofa slobs get less action than guys on the move.

3. Stay young

Remind him that a healthy lifestyle helps you enjoy a longer life and you want him to be around for you and your family. It's not all nut loaves and a glass of milk. Healthy living, a good, varied diet and plenty of exercise keeps you younger and more active. Prevention is better than cure – yes, it's a cliché, but it's also true.

4. Keep up

Keep track of the necessary medical check-ups, including blood pressure and cholesterol, as well as the latest research on diseases that particularly affect men – heart disease, prostate and testicular cancer. If he is really scared of going to the doctor, make an appointment for you both to have your regular tests together.

Mind Your Man's Midriff

Does your man have the belly of a beer drinker, the abs of an athlete and abstainer, the muscle tone of – well, a mussel – flabby, wobbly, uncooked and to some, unappetising, or the six-pack of a serial cruncher? When it comes to his tummy, can you 'pinch an inch'? Or is it more a case of 'grab a handful'?

Let's take the lid (and the shirt) off the whole issue of the midriff – if you and he can stomach it of course.

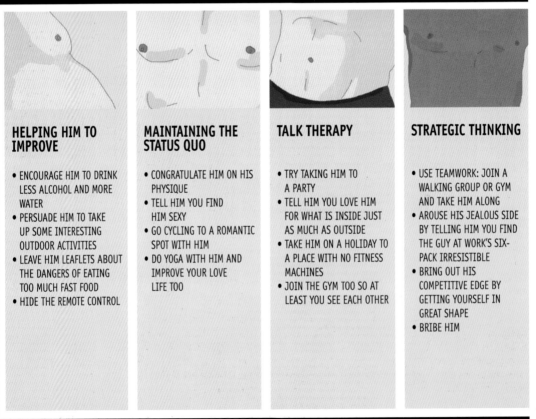

MANagement Techniques

HELPING HIM TO IMPROVE

- ENCOURAGE HIM TO DRINK LESS ALCOHOL AND MORE WATER
- PERSUADE HIM TO TAKE UP SOME INTERESTING OUTDOOR ACTIVITIES
- LEAVE HIM LEAFLETS ABOUT THE DANGERS OF EATING TOO MUCH FAST FOOD
- HIDE THE REMOTE CONTROL

MAINTAINING THE STATUS QUO

- CONGRATULATE HIM ON HIS PHYSIQUE
- TELL HIM YOU FIND HIM SEXY
- GO CYCLING TO A ROMANTIC SPOT WITH HIM
- DO YOGA WITH HIM AND IMPROVE YOUR LOVE LIFE TOO

TALK THERAPY

- TRY TAKING HIM TO A PARTY
- TELL HIM YOU LOVE HIM FOR WHAT IS INSIDE JUST AS MUCH AS OUTSIDE
- TAKE HIM ON A HOLIDAY TO A PLACE WITH NO FITNESS MACHINES
- JOIN THE GYM TOO SO AT LEAST YOU SEE EACH OTHER

STRATEGIC THINKING

- USE TEAMWORK: JOIN A WALKING GROUP OR GYM AND TAKE HIM ALONG
- AROUSE HIS JEALOUS SIDE BY TELLING HIM YOU FIND THE GUY AT WORK'S SIX-PACK IRRESISTIBLE
- BRING OUT HIS COMPETITIVE EDGE BY GETTING YOURSELF IN GREAT SHAPE
- BRIBE HIM

Abs or Flab?

Bob the Beer Drinker

Bob has what is loosely (over his belt) called a beer drinker's potbelly. Not to be confused with a pot-holing belly, as he would get stuck in too many. He has a poor diet, largely liquid-based, and he is allergic to exercise (it brings him out in a nervous sweat). He watches what he eats, first on television and then on his plate, and he is very much an ads man, a fast-food guy, a shaker when he moves. He needs to become more of an abs man, a slower food guy and a mover not a shaker. Remember, too much abdominal fat in men is potentially dangerous and can lead to all sorts of complications.

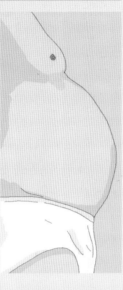

Andy the Ab-Solutioner

Andy is a mover – he exercises, watches what he eats (lots of fruit and vegetables, fish, chicken and nuts rather than cookies), moderates his alcohol intake and indulges in cardiovascular activity. He walks to work, runs home, cycles to the shops, plays sport with friends. He is an all-rounder, but not in the Bob sense. He does bicycle crunches at home, reverse curls in his lunch hour, and in the evenings relaxes and stays supple with yoga. His abdominal muscles are strong, thereby supporting his back, protecting his internal organs, aiding his lungs to breathe and helping his posture.

Chris the Compulsive Cruncher

Chris is an 'obsessive compulsive'. He goes to the gym more than the office. He just loves machines and has more in his apartment than chairs or tables. His sofa has a pulley system with dumbbells. He pulls more weights than dates. He eats for bulk. His biceps bulge more than his address book. He knows the names and circumference-to-mass ratio of every muscle, but he needs reminding about the names or birthdays of his friends and colleagues. He has a washboard as flat as his conversation. Chris needs to moderate his exercise regime and pepper it with social niceties. He needs to tone down.

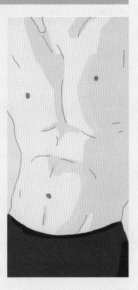

No Muscle, Tone

Tony – or Tone, as he is addressed with irony by some – has a stomach that looks rather like an unpainted canvas. It lacks definition; it is unfinished business, uncharted territory, an incomplete, hardly even begun, sculpture. No-Tone is not overweight but undertoned. He drinks and eats in moderation, and quite sensibly, but does little exercise and is a stranger to bicycle crunches, reverse curls and press-ups. He walks, but only if necessary and never with a spring in his step; he runs, but only to catch a bus or a train or hail the last cab on the rank. He needs to tone up and firm up.

The 6 Habits of a Successful Health Promoter

If your man doesn't take his health seriously or treat his own body (never mind yours) with the respect it deserves, then you may have to step in. You will soon have him eating out of your hands. Similarly, many guys go pale and sweaty at the very mention of the word 'doctor'. You may have to try and convince them that a healthy lifestyle is generally a longer one, that being ill is not a sign of weakness and that knowledge and preventative action are vital. If he puts it off until tomorrow, there may be fewer tomorrows.

Wall to Wall

TRY A FEW FACTS OUT ON HIM:

- WOMEN LIVE LONGER THAN MEN.

- WOMEN DRINK AND SMOKE LESS THAN MEN.

- MORE WESTERN MEN DIE OF HEART DISEASE THAN WOMEN.

- THERE ARE MORE OBESE MEN THAN OBESE WOMEN. HMMM, THE ANSWER IS IN THE BALANCE.

- WOMEN ARE BETTER AT MULTI-TASKING THAN MEN. NOT REALLY RELEVANT, BUT TRUE ALL THE SAME.

You can make simple but effective changes to your lifestyle with relative ease and lack of drama. He may not even notice until his trousers fall down (because he has lost weight, of course).

Good nutrition

Eat more of the healthy foods at the bottom of the pyramid, and fewer of the unhealthy ones at the top.

Get fruity

'An apple a day keeps the doctor away.' It's a cliché but it should appeal to him. The only doctors he knows well are on *ER*. Eating five or more pieces of fruit and vegetables a day and less saturated fat can really improve your man's health and may reduce the risk of cancer and other chronic diseases. Slip a banana into his lunchbox (not that one!). Munch on blueberries (good for bad cholesterol) and strawberries (may help maintain good eyesight for longer) together in the evening. Much better than cookies. Use raw veggies for dips instead of crisps. Think of all the vitamins, minerals and fibre he will be getting and all the extra energy he will have…

Go nuts

If your guy gets regular snack attacks, try handing him nuts (careful how you say that). Peanuts, for example, are high in antioxidants, the chemicals that can help protect against cancer and heart disease and block the ageing effects of free radicals, those pesky unstable molecules that damage living cells. They are also high in healthy monounsaturated fats. Almonds are a good source of protein and of vitamin E, which helps fight heart disease. Walnuts are good for you, too. Don't just add nuts to your usual diet. You need to try and replace the baddies with the goodies. Fill the cookie tin with a selection of nuts and dried fruit for starters. Sprinkle nuts and a dash of olive oil on salads instead of a heap of mayo.

Take the weight off his feet

If your guy is overweight or obese he runs an increased risk of diseases and conditions such as diabetes, high blood pressure, heart disease and strokes. Try to persuade him to eat more fresh food than pre-packaged meals. The odd take-out is OK, but a regular diet of processed food is not good for either of you. The packaging may claim to contain food that is low in fat but it could be high in salt and additives. Why not spend an evening cooking a nice meal using fresh produce? Teach him some of your healthy chicken and fresh fish recipes and show him how easy they are to prepare. Share a few of your kitchen tricks as things steam up. You could even try a bit of hot yoga.

Get him moving

All it takes is about 30 minutes of aerobic exercise three days a week to keep fit. Do it together. Just you, your man and the big outdoors (or indoors if it just too horrid out there). If you want to lose weight, you can burn 1,000 calories a week with 30 minutes a day. So don't sit on your butt, shake it about.

Why not arrange a different activity for each day of the week? Monday, swimming. Tuesday, skipping. Wednesday, jogging. Thursday, join him at a boxing class. Friday, dancing. Saturday, yoga or a candle-lit massage. Sunday, a walk to the pub (but no cab home). It doesn't need cash, just a bit of commitment.

Build up to the big burn. Don't start Olympic training day one or he will be having an early bath and be back on the substitute bench before you can say 'groin strain'. Do consult your doctor before embarking on a strict exercise regime.

Cut it out and cut it down

There's no nice way of saying this. Stop smoking. It is linked with lung cancer and heart disease. If he smokes and you don't, he is putting you at risk, too. And vice versa. Try to support your guy in quitting – completely rather than slowly. Do it together as a joint challenge if you both smoke, but maybe not just before a big presentation or particularly stressful week at work. Encourage, congratulate and divert him. Arrange a weekend away if he manages the first month cigarette-free.

Try to cut down his alcohol consumption if he is regularly drinking over 21 units a week (it's 14 for you by the way and the same for him if he has high blood pressure). Stock up on low-alcohol beers and interesting mineral waters. Get him to write a drink diary – he can then see just how much he is drinking per week. Do the same. It could come as a surprise. Binge drinking is both dangerous and its effects (both long and short term) unattractive.

Lose The Booze

The phrase to remember here is: B.I.N.G.E.

B O Y S
I N E B R I A T E D
N O
G I R L S
E N T I C E D

Explain this to your man, and try to persuade him that he doesn't have to hit the bottle too hard or too often. Moderate drinking is OK – it may even be good for you, cutting the risk of heart attacks according to some research. However, the excessive intake of alcohol can affect just about every organ in your body. Brain cells are destroyed, and weight gain, depression, impotence and mood swings can result.

As if that isn't enough, regular heavy drinking can also permanently damage the liver, heart and pancreas, as well as exacerbating any existing health problems. All in all, it simply isn't worth it.

Doctor Who?

Encourage your guy to research his family medical history and discover any conditions that may be hereditary. If problems are found early, treatment and cure have much better chances of success. Routine examinations and screenings are important, but just getting him to the surgery could be a challenge in itself. Do some research on your local healthcare provider and if he is reluctant to go, suggest you visit together to find out about necessary, routine check-ups.

1

Get him to keep a record of his vaccinations, particularly if he travels regularly. When did he last have a tetanus jab? When did you for that matter?

2

Lend him your high-factor sunscreen. Everyone needs protection against the harmful rays of the sun. The sun's not sexist – it is damages us all.

3

Some men keep their toothbrushes for months, so encourage him to get one the next time he's out shopping. Remind him that Floss is not the cat's name.

4

Ask Santa or his Mum to buy him a juicer or blender for his birthday so he can drink fresh fruit for breakfast. Come up with some good concoctions – carrot and ginger, banana and orange with a couple of strawberries and so on. Add a bit of ginseng for extra activity...

5

Buy him a wok for healthy stir-fries using chicken and fresh vegetables in different, tasty sauces.

6

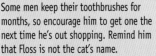

Hide the pizza delivery phone number, and chuck out take-away menus as soon as they arrive.

Check-up

An annual MOT is a good idea, but for specific conditions he may need a health check more often. Stress the routine angle, but don't make him panic.

Some men are hypochondriacs, others feel they should push through the pain. Try to work out if he is exaggerating or ignoring his condition.

7

Bribe him to take the take-outs out of his diet by saying you will take him out instead, maybe to that new sushi bar in town.

8

Go on a cookery or yoga course together. Share the health and the wealth. Fitness doesn't come by stealth.

9

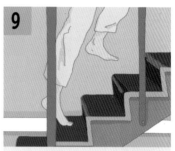

Tell him how many calories you can lose running up stairs – and that's before you've got to the bedroom...

10

Set him a challenge and he may rise to the bait. Sponsor him to do a charity walk or swim, or even a half marathon.

11

Buy a big Pilates ball and exercise whilst watching television – even he shouldn't find that too much of a multi-tasking challenge.

12

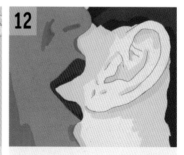

Tell him how much better he looks as he gets healthier. Flattery works wonders in men...

Face Facts

Have you ever noticed how many couples look like each other? What women find attractive about men varies considerably, which is nature's way of ensuring that one man doesn't get all of the girls! Picture all the men you have found attractive. Spot any similarities? Read on to find out why this may have been.

Hair

Check out a chap's coiffure. A good mop of hair can be very attractive, but a nice smooth bald head indicates an extra supply of testosterone, so there are compensations. The hair types you go for will inevitably depend on your personal preferences, but there are a few factors to consider. If a man is at ease with his hair, he is likely to be at ease with himself. Wigs, mullets, pieces, extensions, ornaments and regular change of colour – all these should be noticed, noted and perhaps used in evidence against a chap. Vanity, insecurity and an identity crisis may play parts. Dirty, greasy hair may be part of a general personal hygiene regime so be warned. If he never takes his baseball cap off, watch out for what lurks beneath.

Eyes

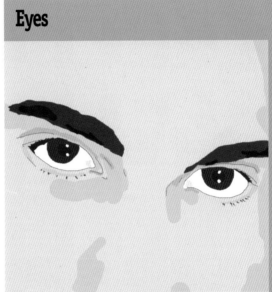

It is what eyes convey that is most important, although men with darker eyes traditionally have the upper hand on the dependable and mature stakes. Whether you prefer dark, blue, green, grey (or even a mixture) is up to you. Look into the eyes and try to see what's going on behind them. Your mission is to conjure up some or all of the following words: kind, sensitive, caring, sharing, loving, considerate, approachable. If the eyes shift from side to side, lurk in middle-distance while you talk or simply never return your gaze, look elsewhere. Large eyes are generally more attractive, but again don't take them at face value. Look for the message within them.

History and Mystery

Women have demanded different qualities from men throughout the ages. Think of our ancient ancestors and contrast this with modern woman. While they were cleaning out the cave and lighting the fires, women wanted their men to be strong and healthy – they needed to act as protectors and providers. Today, the requirements are different, and some women want men to be in touch with their softer side. Clearly, this will affect the features that they find attractive.

Lips

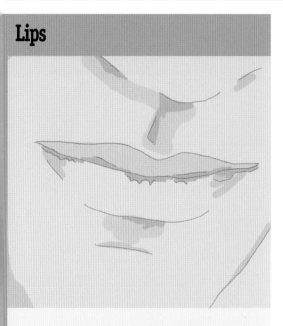

A mouth that is sensual, full, generous, potentially passionate, yet at the same time macho and rugged is the ideal. That may be asking too much of the average guy, but beware thin, mean lips – they get the thumbs down, particularly those that are no more than a dark doodle. Look for lips that are middle to full in size and plumpness, rather than middle to mean. Don't pay lip service to them. Lips express warmth, receptivity and sensuality. Interestingly they become redder in colour and fuller in appearance when their owner is excited so this is a useful signal upon which to focus. Pursed and puckered lips may convey both disapproval and disinterest on the sexual front.

Nose

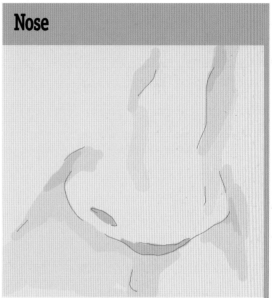

Sadly for Pinocchio, the link between the size of a man's nose and the size of his 'appendage' is a myth. And, what's more, it would be too much of a temptation for guys to lie. Scientists have found that the nose does indeed increase both in size and temperature during love-making but that's where the link ends. A strong nose can be appealing in a man – the proboscis monkey takes it a little far with his enormous, pendulous and fleshy appendage, but girl monkeys love it. A broken nose may indicate sporting prowess or an enjoyment of fights, and a button nose is OK if in harmony with the rest of the features. Look for a right-left balance, which our instincts tell us reflect a capacity for being healthy.

How to Read a Ventriloquist

Men use body signals a great deal – in the office, in the car, in the home, in the car salesroom, in the pub. Here's a DIY Decoder to various signals you may have to try and interpret. It's a Guyway code:

The Guyway Code:

I AM CONFIDENT

I'M RELAXED ABOUT MYSELF AND IN TOUCH WITH MY OWN VALUE, BUT ALSO A LITTLE ARROGANT AND MAYBE A TOUCH SUPERIOR.

I AM SO BORED

I'M CLOSING DOWN, CUTTING OFF, AND I'M NOT GOING TO ALLOW ANYTHING TO PERSUADE ME TO LISTEN. GET ME OUT OF HERE...

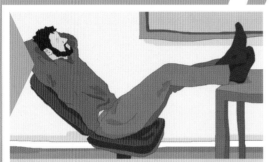

I AM RELAXED

MY HANDS ARE BEHIND MY BACK, AND SO ARE NOT CREATING A BARRIER BETWEEN US. NOW WOULD BE A GOOD TIME TO ASK ME FOR A FAVOUR. GO FOR IT – ASK FOR A NEW CAR.

I AM SO PLEASED TO SEE YOU

I AM MAKING EXTRA PHYSICAL CONTACT BY TOUCHING YOU ON THE SHOULDER WHILE SHAKING HANDS. I AM EXPRESSING PLEASURE AT SEEING YOU. I MAY EVEN KISS YOU.

I AM VERY CONFUSED

I'M SCRATCHING MY HEAD AS IF IT WERE MY BRAIN, DESPERATELY TRYING TO WORK OUT WHAT IT IS YOU ARE SAYING/ASKING/COMMUNICATING.

I DON'T LIKE WHAT YOU'RE SAYING

I'M CREATING A VERY OBVIOUS BARRIER BETWEEN US. I'M IN DEFENSIVE MODE AND YOU WOULDN'T LIKE WHAT I'M THINKING.

WELCOME TO MY CASTLE

I'M WELCOMING YOU WITH OPEN ARMS – QUITE LITERALLY. I'M USHERING YOU INTO MY WORLD. DID YOU BRING YOUR TOOTHBRUSH?

LET ME REASSURE YOU

I'M TOUCHING YOU INSIDE YOUR INTIMATE SPACE. I'M EXPRESSING MY DESIRE PHYSICALLY. I'M VERY KEEN TO MAKE A MOVE ON YOU.

Nil by Mouth Seduction Technique

If you are no good at learning new languages, don't worry. Male body language is pretty ancient (if not caveman) stuff, and if you do your homework and study what follows, you will come out on top. Interpreting male behaviour will become second nature. Just think **MATE** – males attempting to expand (their family tree), or **SOS** – Sway, ogle, swagger. Seduction or singledom is the male mantra.

Seduction or Singledom

HERE'S THE ESSENTIAL GUIDE TO WHAT MEN DO, AND THE ORDER THEY DO IT IN:

- LOOK FOR A MATE
- SPOT A MATE
- MAKE SURE SHE SPOTS YOU
- DATE THE MATE
- MATE WITH THE MATE
- LOVE THE MATE
- LIVE WITH THE MATE
- STAY UP LATE WITHOUT THE MATE

Step 1: He spots you

When a man sees a woman he is attracted to, he is likely to preen. This will involve fiddling with his clothing and hair – he may straighten his tie, smooth his collar or arrange some other item of clothing in order to smarten up his act. He will then touch his hair, smoothing it down or ruffling it, depending on which look he feels is more attractive.

Step 2: He checks you out

Now watch his eyes. He will look at you – maybe once or twice – and then he will try to hold your gaze. If shy, he might give you a semi-sideways glance. His eyebrows may take on a life of their own, moving up and down mime-artist style, and his pupils will dilate with the adrenaline released by sheer excitement tinged with fear, although distance may make this hard to notice. You should be able spot if his lips part slightly. If he licks his lips, you may want to move away quickly.

His eyes will travel between yours and your upper torso (aka above your belt) and back up again – a Bermuda triangle into which he hopes to sail his boat and drop anchor but from which he may never return. Step 2 has just taken place.

Step 3: He shows you what he's made of

Now watch his body. He might put his hands on his hips, suggesting that he is open and available. Look out for his thumbs in his belt or the pocket of his jeans. This is the equivalent of a neon light pointing at his genitals. An Elvis-like pelvis movement could accompany this. He might spread his legs and point his foot in your direction. If all of these occur, then he finds you pretty attractive. A quick shoulder shrug could be an attempt to look 'bigger' if he is needs to add height to his physique. If short he will try to look wider in order to fox you. It's an ASS thing (arch, stretch, swivel). You've just seen step 3.

Step 4: He wants to touch you

He may fondle a part of his own body (his earlobe, for example). This is indicates which of your body parts he would like to play with. Similarly, he may copy your gestures – some call this a mimic gesture, others call it a reflex reflect thing. If you stroke your nose, he will caress his own. This means he is on your hook. If he picks it, sling yours. Step 4 is in progress.

He has noticed you, he likes what he sees and he is communicating that in his best body language. Make sure you are all eyes (rather than ears).

PERFECT PETER

Turn to page 132 for lots of tips on how to do the flirting bit once you have spotted a potential date.

Step 5: The engagement

No, not that sort or engagement! We're not talking 'down on one knee and out with a diamond ring' here. Not unless you are both really fast movers, anyway. More likely than a spontaneous proposal of marriage is that he will try to engage you in conversation.

This is a crucial moment. It is your first chance to make your mind up about this one – you can either talk, or walk. Let's assume you choose to talk. As he speaks, he will try to hold your gaze (or your hand, if he's very forward). At the very least he will keep glancing at you in order to check if you are still interested in what he's got to say. (He will also want to keep checking that you are still in the room.) If he asks you to dance, watch his movements (to find out what they reveal, see the panel below).

Seduction on the Dance Floor

He may not know it, but the first dance can be a make-or-break situation. While he's worrying about whether his hair looks OK or if his flies are undone, you need to keep your eyes open and your wits about you. Dancing can also get pretty intimate, so taking the appropriate steps here is essential.

- **Keep an eye on how your dance partner moves. Lots of pelvic thrusts and hip-hurling are a sure-fire indication of what he has in mind for later.**

- **Few men possess the natural rhythm of Elvis or the snake-hipped genius of Tom Jones, but they all think they do. Just try not to laugh...**

- **For a real smooth mover, dancing can be a powerful seduction tool. Be on your guard – unless you want to save the last dance for him.**

Read his Body and his Face

Men often complain that they need to be mind readers to be able to understand women, but maybe they should just try to be a little more observant and they wouldn't get themselves into so much trouble. Help on how you can read his mind comes later, but in the meantime this section may help you to read some things that are equally important: his body and his face.

Defensive

If a man is on the defensive he will, quite literally, defend his body by crossing his arms and, on occasion, his legs too. Some men put their hands over their genitals, but this is rather an extreme reaction and more likely to be seen on the soccer pitch. He will step back, putting a distance between you. His eyes may narrow and little, if any, direct eye contact will be made. He may seek refuge behind sunglasses if feeling really defensive. His hips will be hunched and closed, his lips thin and sealed, his body closed for business. My body is my castle and I defend it. Cross the moat at your own peril. Got the message? Try echoing his body language if he is drawn or difficult – he may open up to you. Well, anything's worth a go.

Deceitful

Wouldn't it be wonderful if we all had lie detectors? In the absence of these, the following may help you verify the veritas (that's Latin for truth, by the way – honest). If a man is spinning a yarn, watch out for telling tell-tale signs. He will make minimal (if any) eye contact. His brow may glisten with nervous sweat, he will develop a dry mouth and indulge in an unattractive chewing action. Involuntary twitching may accompany his web of deceit. He may stutter, shift from foot to foot, rub his nose, stroke his chin, scratch his eyebrow, cover his mouth or fake a smile (read on if you want to know how to spot one). All he needs is a T-shirt saying 'I'm a liar.' But you would have to buy that. Think shifty, squirmy, sweaty and you are on the right track.

In the Mood

Posture, gesture and touch all play key roles in how we express ourselves, the messages we give out (intentionally or otherwise) and how we interact with those around us.

Keeping a keen eye on these three aspects will help you to stay one step ahead when it comes to assessing what your man is really thinking and feeling.

Angry

An angry man may well use aggressive body language before, after or during his rather more verbal expression of mood. He may invade your space, thereby asserting his right to cross the personal distance threshold and, at the same time, make himself look taller (by being closer – it's not that sophisticated). Hands on hips will make him look wider and ready for battle. He may lock you in a threatening stare that says 'Me predator, you prey.' His face will go white, his lips will be compressed and he may even snarl. Verbal communication usually accompanies anger but finger-pointing is often involved in an attempt to signal dominance. He may clasp the back of his own neck in an attempt to control his rage. If he clenches his fists and jerks his chin upwards, watch out.

Happy

Happiness is a more obvious condition to spot. A happy man's body will relax, his face will look as if he has had a temporary face lift – a big smile will open up his features, his eyes will express joy and crinkle at the edges, showing his crow's feet. Faking happiness in the eye area is very hard to do, and you can tell a genuine from a contrived smile by seeing how long it lasts – a fake smile lingers just a little too long, while a real one is shorter-lived. However radiant the smile, a drooping of the corners of the mouth will give him away. A happy man may raise his arms and punch the air (as if he has scored a goal or won the lottery). His body will open, expressing joy and a release of the moat bridge. Laughter will accompany the gesture and some men may even howl with hyena-like enthusiasm.

 # Emotional ID

Size Doesn't Matter
The male brain is larger than the female brain, but of no greater intellectual capacity. It's just men obsessed with size, as usual...

Chalk and Cheese
In this chapter we get inside their heads and discover that men and women really do think differently. We were right all along – naturally.

More than Words
Men talk less than women – their phone bills are certainly lower. But they are still thinking when they are silent (or so they would like us to believe).

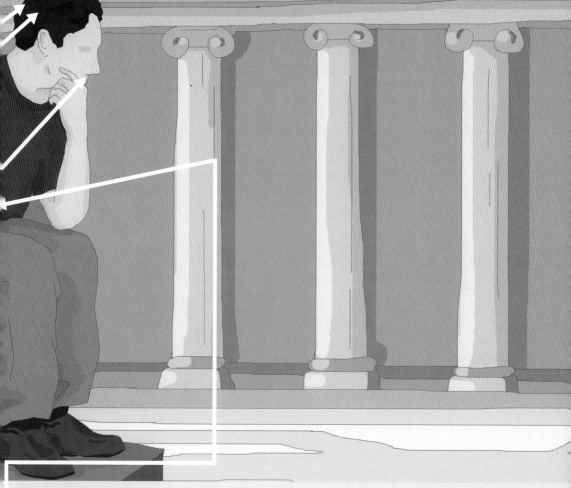

'Put Einstein's brain in Hercules's body and add Groucho Marx's sense of humour. The perfect male cocktail.'
ANNABEL PILKINGTON, 1970

The Second Brain
A good diet isn't just about staying (or getting) slim. Food also has a major impact on our mental health and general sense of well being.

Chercher La Femme

Now let's try to get inside men's heads and check out what they are thinking. It seems that male brains are larger than those of females by up to about 10%. However, before you spread this statistic and inflate egos even more, it is worth noting that men are generally larger than women physically, and there is apparently a link between size of mammal and brain size. The important thing to remember is that a seriously weighty issue is preying constantly on their minds – sex. They need to check out the environment to find an appropriate mate – a ritual that dates way back to when genes were genes and not jeans, when loincloths not Levi's were the order of the day and before aftershave was invented.

This preoccupation with procreation may well account for men's celebrated skills at map-reading and their excellent visual-spatial skills. They are constantly aiming at a particular target, looking for an ultimate destination – whether it is Flingtown, Partnersville, Wifeshire or Kids'r'us City. Procreate to prosper – it's a simple survival issue. The world is charted by maps leading to potential partners, and we all know how good men are at reading them. The office, the bar, the club, the beach – they scan all of these with their in-built GPS (Girl Positioning System) to pinpoint their potential prey and calculate the quickest, safest way to procure it.

It appears that men and women use their brains differently. Men tend to be more focused and concentrate on a particular issue or problem, whereas females are more inclined to look at the bigger picture. This may well go back to when men had to focus on making wild beasts into the family dinner without becoming theirs first.

Men and women tend to be better at different things, language being one of them. Women are good at words. They communicate in order to establish a relationship with others, to get closer or to bond with them. Men generally communicate to convey specific information or to establish their status in a group. They complain that women use a paragraph when a sentence will do and can find listening at length challenging. On the other hand, women wonder when someone is going to publish a dictionary of grunts and shrugs. Men and women communicate for different reasons – read on to discover more.

PERFECT PETER

This section discusses some of the instincts of the male species, but to really get inside his head, see page 46.

Questionnaire

Check out the following questions to see how you and your man communicate at the moment. You could even do the questionnaire together to see if your answers are the same, similar or totally different.

DO YOU FIND COMMUNICATING WITH YOUR MAN:

A) AN IMPOSSIBLE TASK MOST OF THE TIME
B) A CHALLENGE FROM TIME TO TIME
C) A NIGHTMARE
D) A DELIGHT
E) A TRIAL

DOES HE LISTEN TO YOU WHEN YOU ARE TALKING:

A) INTENTLY
B) INTERMITTENTLY
C) IMPERCEPTIBLY
D) INTERRUPTEDLY
E) INTUITIVELY

DO YOU THINK YOU REALLY UNDERSTAND EACH OTHER:

A) MOST OF THE TIME
B) ALL OF THE TIME
C) RARELY
D) VERY OCCASIONALLY
E) FROM TIME TO TIME

DOES HE INTERRUPT YOU MORE OFTEN THAN YOU INTERRUPT HIM:

A) YES
B) NO
C) YES YOU DO
D) NO I DON'T
E) YES YOU DO

DOES YOUR MAN NEED TO HAVE 'QUIET TIME' DURING WHICH HE DOESN'T SPEAK MUCH:

A) REGULARLY
B) NEVER
C) OCCASIONALLY
D) HE WOULD NOT DREAM OF IT
E) ONLY IF PROMPTED BY YOU

WHEN YOU TALK TO YOUR PARTNER WHILE HE IS WATCHING THE TELEVISION, DOES HE:

A) LISTEN AND REPLY POLITELY
B) COMPLETELY IGNORE YOU
C) TELL YOU TO HUSH
D) TURN UP THE VOLUME
E) RESPOND WITH A GRUNT

DO YOU FIND IT HARD TO DISCUSS YOUR PROBLEMS WITH HIM:

A) ALL OF THE TIME
B) REGULARLY
C) SOMETIMES
D) RARELY
E) NEVER

WHOM WOULD HE PREFER TO TALK TO IF HE HAD AN EMOTIONAL ISSUE:

A) YOU
B) HIS MOTHER
C) HIS FATHER
D) HIS BEST MATE
E) HIS DOG

Different Reasons to Communicate

Men and women communicate in different ways and for different reasons. Interestingly, it seems that when presented with a challenge, women are more likely to use both sides of their brains, whereas a man tends to employ only those parts he feels best suited to resolve the issue. Men appear to listen to language using the left side of the brain, whereas women use both sides. Let's start by examining why men communicate.

Different Ways of Communication

Men

- TO CONVEY INFORMATION
- TO DISCOVER FACTS
- TO GIVE ORDERS
- TO ESTABLISH STATUS
- TO GAIN CONTROL
- TO ORDER A BEER
- TO FIND OUT THE SCORE
- TO SCORE

Women

- TO DELIVER INFORMATION
- TO RECEIVE INFORMATION
- TO DISCOVER INFORMATION
- TO SHARE A PROBLEM
- TO EXPLORE EMOTION
- TO EMPATHISE
- TO ESTABLISH A BOND
- TO GAIN TRUST
- TO FEEL BETTER
- TO RESOLVE A PROBLEM
- TO GOSSIP
- TO GIGGLE
- TO LAUGH
- TO MAKE OTHERS LAUGH
- TO TALK ABOUT HOW DIFFICULT IT IS TO DEAL WITH MEN

The lists shown left are glaringly different both in content and length – rather like the shopping lists of men and women about to do their Christmas shopping. It would appear that men and women speak very different languages. One way for women to bridge this verbal gulf is to learn to talk Manspeak (and vice versa of course – the guys don't get off that lightly), even if it involves learning to interpret silence. It seems that generating words is one of many female talents, but if men are only employing one side of their brains when listening, the equation could present quite a challenge. However, given half a chance and half an ear or brain (his not yours) and more than half a mind to learn a new language, success should be within reach. It won't be long before women are bilingual. Learning a foreign language is an excellent way of keeping your mind active and alert, so there are other benefits, too. A spot of bridge-building is all that is required. Bring the verbal bricks and supports to the task and two-way traffic will soon flow.

Let's eyeball the men

Men and women communicate with each other and themselves in very different ways. Research has shown that if you put a group of women in a room, they are much more likely to talk face to face, with lots of eye contact, gathering in small groups or one big, democratic circle. They will soon start talking about something of communal interest; they will exchange experiences, offer advice to each other and display early signs of friendship and bonding. They will take it in turns to talk. A group of men, on the other hand, are much less likely to make such immediate eye contact and will probably stand in a row, eyeing each other up surreptitiously to assess who is the alpha male. They will tend to discuss concrete facts, such as whose soccer team is the best, whose car is fastest, who has got the best laptop and how the price of beer is going up.

Men at work – interrupting

Research has also shown that if you put both sexes in a more formal arena, such as a mixed discussion group or a workshop with a facilitator, the men are much more likely to dominate the conversation and tend to interrupt the women rather than be interrupted by them. Men hold the floor while women hold their tongue. It seems that men see talking as a way of establishing their status and credentials within the group. Men are more likely to contribute facts and opinion ('The fact is, I think I am right…') whereas women will make supportive and encouraging comments ('I think that was an interesting point…'). Women, the research shows, talk more in social contexts and men take the lead verbally in more formal arenas.

Strong, silent types

Silence can be golden, as the saying goes. And for some the strong, silent type is very alluring. Silence can make men seem more enigmatic, mysterious, even respectful, and it can hint at hidden,

unplumbed depths. Silence in others can be less appealing. If your man comes home after a hard day and turns into a sofa slob, glued inextricably and wordlessly to the television, he may be recharging. Like his phone, he is plugged into an external power source in order to boost his communication potential. So if you are desperate to talk about your own day, it might be worth waiting for his batteries to be charged up before you do. Read the signals and call a girlfriend or your mother in the meantime – or chat to the dog.

The Sounds of Silence

When men are silent, women conjure up a host of reasons why this might be.

She thinks:

- HE DOESN'T LOVE ME
- HE IS BORED WITH ME
- HE DOESN'T HAVE ANYTHING TO SAY TO ME
- WE HAVE NOTHING IN COMMON
- HE IS THINKING OF SOMEONE ELSE
- HE IS PLANNING HOW TO DUMP ME
- HE IS HAVING AN AFFAIR
- HE IS UNHAPPY
- HE HATES ME
- I AM NO GOOD AT RELATIONSHIPS
- I DON'T UNDERSTAND HIM
- I CAN'T BEAR IT WHEN HE IS MOODY
- HE'S SOOOOOO DULL

In fact, men are probably thinking something completely different.

He thinks:

- I WONDER IF I WILL GET A BONUS THIS YEAR
- HOW LONG TILL I CAN HAVE A BEER?
- I CAN'T LET ON THAT I DON'T KNOW THE ANSWER
- THIS IS A REALLY GREAT MATCH ON TELEVISION
- I WISH I HAD BEEN A FAMOUS FOOTBALLER
- WHAT WOULD I BUY IF I WON THE LOTTERY?
- SHOULD I GO FOR SILVER OR BLACK WHEN I GET A NEW CAR?
- WHY DO WOMEN FEEL THEY HAVE TO TALK ALL THE TIME?
- HOW DO WOMEN TALK AND WATCH A DVD AT THE SAME TIME?
- THAT NEW GIRL IN THE OFFICE IS QUITE ATTRACTIVE
- WHAT CAN I GET MY GIRLFRIEND FOR HER BIRTHDAY?
- WHEN IS HER BIRTHDAY?
- WILL SHE WEAR HER BIRTHDAY SUIT?

How to be a Man Whisperer

The basic principles and grammar of Manspeak need studying before any real fluency in the language can be achieved. The following key points will help you understand some of the rules:

15 Ways to Whisper

1 MEN would rather fix your problem or offer a solution than talk at length about it.

2 MEN listen with only a percentage of their brains, but they are still listening.

3 MEN don't like discussing relationship issues – they think you are blaming them for any problems.

4 MEN think that talking about problems means you hold them responsible for them.

5 MEN think words are overrated. They are not always their favourite communication tool.

6 If a MAN is not talking about the issue, it doesn't mean he isn't trying to resolve it.

7 MEN don't want you to offer to solve the problem. They want to find the answer themselves.

8 MEN may withdraw to resolve a problem, unaware of how this may make you feel left out of the equation.

9 Silence is a form of communication for MEN.

10 Sometimes, MEN are literally 'at a loss for words.'

11 MEN stay silent in order to be or appear to be brave and courageous and manly.

12 MEN find it harder than women to ask for support.

13 MALE non-verbal communication as a form of language can be eloquent in its own way. Make an effort to learn body language or you could end up speaking in tongues.

14 MEN feel much more at home doing than speaking, fixing rather than discussing how to fix, planning rather than talking about drawing up a plan.

15 MEN have a tape playing inside their heads with a limited 'interest' time for registering information. Once it is full, it will simply start to rewind.

Talk the talk (or what not to say)

Don't ask a man to do something again and again. Repeating yourself reduces the chances of a task being completed. He will tune out eventually. Once bored, a man can switch off his brain, his ability to hear, and most of all, his willingness to do (if not live). Nagging is more likely to provoke anger rather than action. Less is more.

Avoid asking a man to do things in the house or with the kids as soon as he comes through the door. Give him a few moments to retreat into his 'man-bubble' where he can unwind, rewind or debrief after a hard day at the office/shops/steering wheel. If you greet him with a 'Hello, now then can you please take out the rubbish?' he may go outside but the trash won't.

Orders and commands don't work. A man is more than likely to refuse to do what you tell him or simply do the opposite. Men don't like being given orders at the best of times. It is just about acceptable if they are being paid to do what somebody else tells them. No need to put your man on the payroll. Turn orders into suggestions. Let him issue his own orders.

Don't list all the things a man hasn't done, either verbally or in written form. 'Here's a list of everything you have never done.' Bad strategy. 'What do you think about drawing up a list of things we need to try to get done by the end of the month?' Much better strategy. A list of tasks (to be finished or unfinished) is like a list of failures to a man, a list of criticisms, not a critical list.

Walk the walk (or what to say)

Explain why it is that you need him to do certain tasks. It may be that you cannot take them on physically, or that you have other demands to meet, so let him know that. He will then realise why you are asking. The nag will have a concrete purpose rather than simply to annoy. Task + purpose + reason = chance of completion + 50%. It is a simple equation.

Be clear about what it is you are asking him to do. If you are not precise about what it is you want, you won't get it. 'We have got to improve this house' is much too big, broad and fuzzy. Think of your ultimate goal as a destination – give him reference points and a time frame and then he can find his way to target using his own planning and map-reading skills.

Ask him to complete one major task at a time and give him a realistic time frame. Remember multi-tasking is not a male strength. As the saying goes, one task at a time, things will go fine. Three tasks in one, nothing gets done. Four tasks on a list, opportunity missed. You may be able to multi-ask and multi-task, but that doesn't mean he can do both or all three, four or five.

If he is successful, or even if he isn't but at least gave it a go, congratulate him. Pat him on the back (metaphorically speaking that is). Reward his efforts. Pump up his pride. Stoke his ego (he's bound to have one). Turn nag into negotiate, and mutter into motivate. Put the frame back into work. Congratulate yourself on an ask well expressed and a task well completed. Positive noises are always more effective than negative ones. It takes one to nag, two to negotiate.

More Sounds of Silence – the Tricky Equation Continues

SILENCE = I'm thinking about you

SILENCE = I'm trying to find an answer to this problem

SILENCE = I'm watching the television

SILENCE = I'm pretending to be asleep

SILENCE = I am asleep

SILENCE = I'm in my 'man-bubble'

SILENCE = I just don't have anything to say

SILENCE = I think I am about to get flu

SILENCE = I shouldn't have had that fifth drink last night

SILENCE = If silence is golden, why don't women like it more?

SILENCE = I wonder if silence is contagious

SILENCE = Women love the strong and silent type

SILENCE = I am speechless with admiration

SILENCE = I am being mysterious

SILENCE = Why don't women like silence?

SILENCE = If I had a hearing device, I could switch it off

SILENCE = Is the match on television tonight?

SILENCE = Where did I put the rest of that sandwich

SILENCE = I wonder if the pub is still open

Listen to Your Man

Try to pick the right moment to have an 'important' conversation with your man. Choosing the right occasion is sometimes just as important as finding the right words. If you start with an aggressive attack, he may become defensive and than aggressive himself. If you fire a shot, he will think a war is about to start and get out all his ammunition. Peace talks don't have a chance when both parties are on red alert. 'Hi honey, how was your day? Before you sit down, we need to talk about our financial future…' Not a good idea. 'Hi, honey, listen we both have hard days so let's just relax.' And then a bit later 'Let me know when is a good time to talk about our finances.' Much better…

It's not easy but the following tips might help:

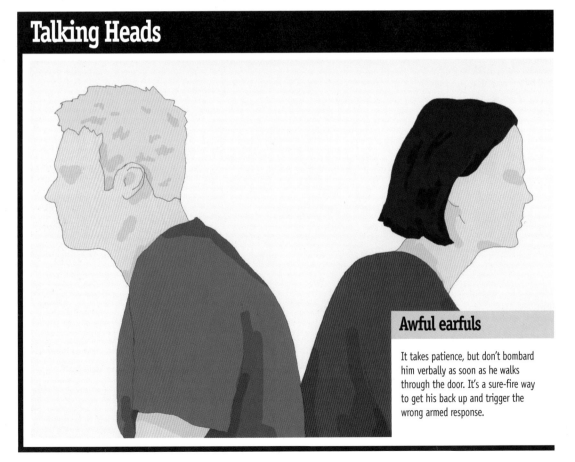

Talking Heads

Awful earfuls

It takes patience, but don't bombard him verbally as soon as he walks through the door. It's a sure-fire way to get his back up and trigger the wrong armed response.

No-No's

The following could lead to a serious communication breakdown:

1. Read the no entry sign

If a man is feeling stressed and in the mood to withdraw to think over a problem, let him have some time and space. Don't try and talk to him about his feelings or suggest solutions until he indicates that he wants you to. He will be in his 'man-bubble'. Don't prick it with your concern or try to enter – it may explode in your face. There's only room for him inside – it's a one-man bubble.

2. Don't waste words

For men, words are functional. They use them principally to convey information or commands. They are not life-giving supplies of oxygen or sources of emotional fulfilment – they are simple tools and messengers. If you have an important piece of information to convey, don't embellish it with descriptive or secondary facts. Want proof? Have a look at the phone bill; who spends more time chatting?

3. Don't push his button

Don't press the boredom button inside a man's head – it operates on a different timer to yours. If you want a man to listen closely to what you are saying, don't forget that his interest level has a limit. The boredom threshold will vary from man to man so test and respect it. Don't exceed the threshold. It's like leaving a 30-minute message on a 20-minute tape. The meaning will simply get lost and something may drop off the end.

4. Don't misread the signals

Don't confuse silence with lack of concern. A man can simply run out of words and may not want to say he can't sort out a problem. Multi-tasking is not one of the male's greatest skills so don't expect him to want to verbalise and organise simultaneously. His brain is ticking even if his mouth isn't moving. Silences can be meaningful both in life and on the stage. Don't make it into a drama. Just exit stage left.

Talk to Your Man

When you next listen to a conversation between a man and a woman, or indeed when you next chat to your man, see whether this apparently sweeping generalisation is actually valid – that men make the statements and women ask the questions. Less surprising is the assertion that women are better listeners (to other women as well as to men, children, bosses and animals) and that they don't interrupt with the same (irritating) frequency as their male counterparts. Conversation interruptus can be annoying, but direct and gentle persuasion against it on your part is required.

Simply getting men to engage verbally is half the challenge. Weird really, as it was no doubt a male Homo Sapiens who uttered the first words ('Who let the fire go out?') thousands of years ago. Hopefully the whole process will become easier and more harmonious if you study a few of the following tips.

Silence Talking

Words of wisdom

Try to use your words to their best effect and remember that less can most definitely be more. This isn't television and you don't get royalties for repeats.

✔ Do-Do's

The following could seriously improve your ability to communicate:

1. Become an interpreter

Broaden your communication skills and become an interpreter. Learn to read the signals as well as understand the words. Sign language demands different talents. A shrug and a grunt may mean he is about to enter or is already ensconced in his 'man-bubble.' It does not necessarily mean he is shrugging you off. Nor should you interpret it as 'Talk to the shoulder 'cos the face ain't listening.'

2. Check the timing

When you really would appreciate talking a matter through with him, ask him when would be a good time and reassure him you are not about to have a go at him. Find a space in the day when you are not going to be interrupted by a soccer match on television or the Miss World contest. He can then prepare himself mentally for the discussion. It's all about good timing.

3. Appreciate his efforts

Make sure that you show your appreciation for making the effort to talk to you. He will then see that communicating can be beneficial for both of you and he will feel positively reinforced. He will appreciate being appreciated. Talk can then be a potential tool. He can see that words can score, and not just home goals. You are both on the same team and it's not about winners and losers.

4. Invent a language

Why not create a private language all of your own? Invent a form of shorthand between yourselves that conveys, in a gently communicative but not challenging or confrontational way, when it's a good time for both parties to chat. 'In or out of the bubble?' 'Sorry, darling, in' might work for you. When you converse with a French person, you speak French (ideally). Shouting English more loudly doesn't work. It's the same with Manspeak.

Inside the Male Brain

What goes on inside the male brain? Now, now, don't be like that. Men only think about sex every few seconds so there's plenty of time for other meaningful thoughts. Men's brains may be larger, but there is no evidence that they are superior. Size doesn't matter at that end of the male species. The brain is a complex organ (in men as well as women) and has still to reveal all its secrets to us. Let's have a look at what has been uncovered and see if it helps us understand guys better. Mask, gloves, scalpel – we're going in.

Brain Hemispheres (Male and Female)

LEFT	RIGHT
CONTROLS RIGHT SIDE OF BODY	**CONTROLS LEFT SIDE OF BODY**
GOOD AT:	**GOOD AT:**

LEFT – GOOD AT:

- CALCULATING
- REASONING
- BEING RATIONAL
- BEING OBJECTIVE
- EXPRESSING LANGUAGE
- ANALYSING
- BEING LOGICAL
- COMPLICATED TASKS
- DETAIL
- DISMANTLING A WHOLE INTO PARTS
  (OR, NOT SEEING THE WOOD FOR THE TREES)
- LISTENING TO LANGUAGE

RIGHT – GOOD AT:

- BEING EMOTIONAL
- UNDERSTANDING EMOTION
- BEING PESSIMISTIC
- BEING SENSITIVE
- OPERATING ON A HUNCH
- CREATIVE TASKS (EG MUSIC)
- INVENTIVE THINKING
- GRASPING THE WHOLE
  (OR, SEEING THE WHOLE WOOD)
- NOT LISTENING

It seems that the left and right hemispheres of the brain (in both males and females) are good at different and particular skills.

Thicker in women

The motorway (the corpus callosum) that links the thinking parts of the two hemispheres is thicker in women, which means they can transfer data between the two hemispheres faster than men. Men tend to be more left-brained, whereas women are thought to have greater access to both sides of the brain. Men use the left side of the brain for language, whereas many women appear to use both sides and tend to be better at communication, understanding and expressing emotion.

Generalising still further, women are better at identifying sound and tone, listening to and empathising with others, being intuitive and nurturing, identifying emotions and responding accordingly, working as part of a team or co-operative, assessing people in a social context and matching things (people, not just shoes and outfits). Talking of shoes, they also have a stronger sense of smell than men. And they can see dust, whereas men can't.

Superior in men

Men are superior in other fields. They are good at mathematical reasoning (paying exactly half on a first date in order not to embarrass you), targeting (beautiful women in a busy bar), distinguishing and spotting things (beautiful women in a very busy bar), rotating an object in their mind's eye (wondering what she would look like when horizontal and reading maps without turning them the right way up), hand-eye co-ordination (hand to ball, beer glass to mouth and so on). Men compartmentalise much more easily than women – they can separate different parts of their lives quite happily. So a woman in every port is a matter of practical convenience rather than a reason to be dumped when discovered.

Men focus on one task at a time whereas women complicate things by juggling a number of issues and priorities, children and work, office and home. They excel at multi-tasking and can even answer questions while watching sport on television.

Why do men get so aggressive?

Women are more likely to use words than actions if threatened by a third party. Women sharpen their verbal weapons and hurl those at their victims rather than physical blows. They tend to be bitchy about someone or exclude them from the group. Men are more likely to use actions, pushing or even hitting the person. It seems that men are innately more aggressive than women (and sometimes we are glad they are), but American research suggests that the part of the brain that modulates aggression is smaller in men than women. Women have better anger-control mechanisms.

Brain Teasers

- IF MEN HAVE BIGGER BRAINS WHY CAN'T THEY DO MORE THINGS AT ONCE?

- IF MEN HAVE BIGGER BRAINS AND BODIES, WHY DOES IT TAKE THEM SO LONG TO DO THE HOUSEWORK?

- IF CAVEMEN DID ALL THE HUNTING, WHY ARE CONTEMPORARY MEN SO BAD AT SHOPPING?

Brain Facts

1. Research has also shown that when men are shown provocative images (i.e. lad's mags), the emotional control centre of their brain, known scientifically as the amygdala but colloquially as the I'm-a-lada, gets much more excited than that of women shown the same sort of naughty pictures. Visual stimulus gets the male brain much more worked up, it seems. This would appear to back up the theory that looks are more important to a man than a woman. Next time you see an beautiful woman on the arm of an unspeakably unattractive male, bear it in mind (better than baring it in mind in this case...).

2. There is some debate about how often the male brain thinks about sex. Some say it is every 7 minutes, others just once a day, and a few claim that men only get round to thinking about it once every few weeks or even months. It is hard for women to know the truth. Try asking your partner what his personal statistic on this score is (if you are interested). See page 32 to identify if he is being economical with the truth. You could offer to give your score too – it might help work out if your mental arithmetic/libido is in synch with his. You may find the results surprising.

3. A brain is about the size of two adult fists side by side. It accounts for only 2% of your body weight but uses about a quarter of your blood supply. Every individual's brain is different. One day we may be able to have brain transplants but in the meantime you can keep yours and his active by learning a new language (try Manspeak for a starter), doing tricky puzzles and quizzes or further research into the male brain. Einstein's brain was certainly unique and has been dissected in an attempt to work out just how.

Male Brain Boxes

Wouldn't it be wonderful to dissect your man's brain and see what is really going on in there – without doing him any irreparable harm, of course. In the years to come, this may be possible. Partners will exchange brain scans instead of phone numbers. In the meantime, and in the hope that this may one day be possible, the following information will help to get you started.

1
Men's brains are about 10% larger than women's, but is it any more significant than their noses or feet being proportionally larger? They smell just the same. A century ago, the French scientist Gustav Le Bon declared that the smaller brains of women explained their 'incapacity to reason' and their 'absence of thought or logic.' Happily, scientists have made progress in their thinking, logic and reasoning since. Most are male but that could be because they are desperately trying to invent female robots.

2
Recent research has discovered that males and females differ in the amount of grey and white matter they have in their brains. It seems too that men and women use the grey and white matter in different degrees when trying to solve problems. So – women do think differently from men, but both sexes are equally intelligent. Or so men think...

3
As we get older our brains get slightly smaller. Men have bigger brains (OK, admit it) but they lose brain tissue sooner than women and in the areas primarily associated with thought and emotion. Men get grumpier with age, so if your youthful guy is already prone to be irritable, be warned – he may well become a grumpy old man. Women tend to become more forgetful as they grow older, which may be good for both parties, as they will forget how much less grumpy their partners used to be.

4

Imaging studies of living brains seem to reveal that when listening, women employ the neurons on both sides of their brain. Men appear to activate those on one side only. Female listening devices also seem to be more attuned naturally – hence women feel like they're on the same wavelength when talking to members of their sex, and keep their 'on' buttons pressed. Men switch off more easily, unless sport is the topic in question.

5

The male brain is compartmentalised and specialised, whereas the female brain is more like an open plan office. Women can see and do a variety of things at the same time. The male brain has separate little rooms, each housing a specific and unrelated task. So for the best outcome, give your man one job at a time. 'He's a man on a mission' – you must have heard that expression. It means exactly what it says. He is completing a task and is consumed completely by it. Don't even try and talk to him.

6

Try talking to a man for more than ten minutes about something intangible like feelings and you may see his eyes glaze over. His powers of concentration will be stretched to the maximum like an elastic band and then go 'ping.' Give him a piece of machinery to dismantle, examine and put together, preferably with lots of buttons and switches, and you won't hear a peep out of him for hours. If you have something really important to say, try writing it on a piece of paper and hiding it inside the machine…

Smart Food, Smart Guy

There is more to eating than meets the eye or the plate. Eating intelligently is an art, or so said the 17th-century moralist Francois de la Rochefoucauld. Yeah, what would he know? Well, four centuries later we are realising that eating certain foods, and avoiding others, can help us not only physically (see page 76) but mentally, too. So don't 'eat your heart out' and try to 'mind what you eat' are accurate instructions, for you and your man. Ever eaten something and felt cross, anxious or sleepy afterwards? Sometimes blood sugar can slump after a big meal along with energy levels, leaving you feeling irritable. Food helps us fight disease and bad moods, too.

Brain Number Two

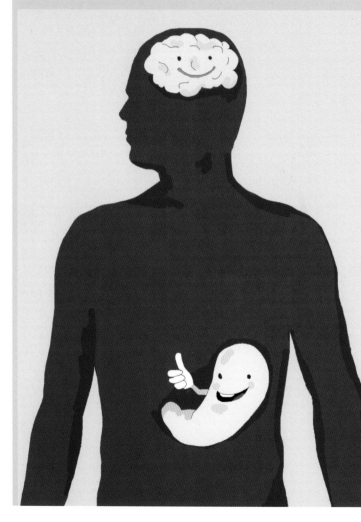

DID YOU KNOW?

- Our gut has its own nervous system with as many nerve connections as the brain and spinal cord put together.

- The gut is like a second brain and secretes chemicals that help it communicate with the rest of our body.

- The stomach's nervous system can react to certain elements in the food and send an email to the brain saying 'Guys, this is making me anxious.' Maybe this happens to your man; maybe you feel he could eat more intelligently.

- Good food equals happy mood. Try to eat for brain power (his and yours).

Good news for chocoholics

Chocolate is a natural anti-depressant and triggers the release of uplifting hormones. That doesn't mean eating a whole box will make either of you deliriously happy.

Top of the morning

The mantra for a top morning is: never miss breakfast. Nutritionists are pretty adamant about this. A healthy start to the day can ensure the rest of it goes well too. Research shows that missing breakfast over an extended period of time can affect behaviour and performance at work or college. Studies worldwide have shown that skipping the first meal of the day can have an adverse effect on physical and mental performance mid-morning and the likelihood of manual accidents increases. Remember, the body has been asleep for several hours without any food intake (unless your guy has Midnight Munch Syndrome and you have Munch Syndrome by proxy). It's important to get the engine moving with quality fuel. Your guy wouldn't get too far in a car with no gas.

Start the day as you mean to go on

When you eat a good breakfast (good does not mean a packet of crisps and a bar of chocolate on the train) energy levels in the body are boosted and the brain has what it needs to fire on all cylinders, too. Breakfast skippers miss out on recommended dietary amounts of vitamins and minerals, particularly iron and calcium. Why not both enjoy a few alcohol-free night-befores and proper breakfast-afters and see how much better your internal engines run.

Without a healthy brekky, we may experience fatigue, loss of concentration, physical and mental exhaustion, and even insomnia. Instead of becoming the friendly roadside recovery agent when your guy's engine packs up, try to encourage him to take out insurance against it. Keep a food diary for a while to see which foods and drinks make you feel good, better, worse.

Too much effort?

Breakfast doesn't have to be a lengthy affair. How long does it take to drink a glass of 100% pure fruit juice? That's one of the 5 portions of fruit sorted already. Tell him an OJ a day keeps one fifth of the doctor away – how is he going to get to you without his lower limbs? A small glass of freshly squeezed juice with lots of pulp is ideal but you may not have time for that every day. An apple or an orange is even better, as you get all the fibre, too.

What you need next are slow-releasing carbohydrates, such as porridge, sprinkled with nuts. If Mr Bear turns his nose up at this, fortified cereal (not the sugar-coated, flavoured sort) and milk (try semi-skimmed) is fine. Milk is good for the body and the mind. It contains vitamin B12, which contributes to the health of brain cells and the nervous system.

No desserts for breakfast

Ideally, breakfast should contain a balance of complex carbohydrates and protein, so grains, dairy and fruit fit the bill. Alternatives include yogurt and fruit or scrambled eggs and a slice of wholemeal toast, but that may have to be for a Sunday, when there is more time (for him) to prepare it. You could boil him a couple of eggs to eat on the go if he is out of the house before you can say 'have you had any break…?' Discourage him from eating desserts for breakfast (sugary things and leftover cake), replace processed white bread with wholemeal bread and go easy on the fat. Save your eggs for the weekend (as it were…). A bag of fruit and nuts and a piece of fruit for those who eat on the hoof is another option.

The DIY breakfast

Make your own muesli and add nuts or shaved coconut. Smoothies are a good choice too, made from semi-skimmed milk and frozen fruit for speed and ease during the week. Get fresh at the weekend. Bought juices and smoothies can contain lots of simple sugars, which head straight to the waistline. You need to handle his love not love his handles, so read the labels and make your own smooth operator.

Caffeine Hit?

To coffee or not to coffee? That is the question. If your man insists on coffee to kick start his brain in the morning, try taking him a cup of hot water and lemon in the shower as the first drink of the day, after which you can unlock the kitchen door and allow him to hit the caffeine. Having switched on his brain, he should not keep it on high alert with endless cups (about three a day is OK) or he may feel anxious and jittery.

The down side of all this caffeine action is that his brain will find it hard to switch off at the end of the day. It's hard to get to sleep if your system has been pumped with gallons of coffee. Beware the large take-out latte or cappuccino on the way to work – it could contain up to 400 calories and lots more fat than you imagine. Semi-skimmed or soya milk are lower in fat.

Brain Savvy – it's a No-Brainer

There's no evidence to show that skipping breakfast will help him (or you) lose weight. In fact, studies show that eating breakfast can kick start the metabolism. Most people who miss out on breakfast tend to eat more food later in the day and are more tempted by snacks than the non-skippers. Break fast or break first (and hit the crisps and cookies at the office). Get him to take healthy snacks to work, such as nuts, sugar-free cereal bars, dried fruit or a natural yogurt. Pop some strawberries, raspberries or cherries into his briefcase or rucksack. Scientists have found that breakfast makes a difference to work-related performance and it can improve alertness and memory, assist with solving problems and help focus minds on the job in hand.

Mind the Menu

GET HIM TO EAT INTELLIGENTLY BY INCLUDING SOME OR ALL OF THE FOLLOWING IN HIS DIET (AND YOURS):

- BANANAS
- PORRIDGE

- WATER (LOTS OF)
- OILY FISH

- FIVE PORTIONS OF FRUIT AND VEGETABLES PER DAY

ALSO, TRY TO LIVE BY THESE THREE SIMPLE RULES;

1. GO EASY ON SATURATED FATS
2. STEAM, GRILL OR STIR-FRY FOOD
3. HAVE A MODERATE ALCOHOL INTAKE

Don't be a banana, eat one

Bananas are full of potassium and vitamin B6 and make a good snack on the way to work or a tasty addition to cereal at breakfast. Bananas are both an aphrodisiac (good for monkeying around) and a happy food. They trigger the release of the neurotransmitter dopamine to make us feel good. They contain fibre (good for constipation and we all know how that can make us grumpy), vitamin C and magnesium and are free of fat, sodium and cholesterol. Great for hangovers, they contain on average around 110 calories and are all-round good eggs.

Calming and cranky carbs

Breakfast cereals supply carbs and these are associated with improved mood. The carbs in our diet supply most of our energy. Simple carbohydrates, as found in refined sugar, syrups and soft drinks for example, fill you up without providing any nutritional value. These 'empty calories' tend to cause greater fluctuation in mood in parallel with fluctuation in blood sugar. Complex carbs, as found in unrefined grains, wholemeal bread, quality cereals and fruit, have a more relaxing effect because they trigger fewer blood sugar disturbances and less release of stress hormones. They supply us with regular, long-term energy. So don't be or eat a sugar-coated jam-packed doughnut first thing in the morning.

Iron out your mood

Iron prevents anaemia, which can lead to fatigue and a lack of concentration. A deficiency can make us irritable and less mentally alert, but a bowl of fortified cereal for brekky or meat and three green veg at night will help supply the required daily allowance.

Water, water, everywhere

Guys should a drink around 2 litres a day to boost mental alertness and energy. If yours emails to say his mind is wandering at work he may be dehydrated (or he may just be distracted by a short skirt). Even mild hydration can lead to headaches and a drop in concentration. Soup, fruit, veg, tea, coffee and unsweetened juices help make up some of this amount.

Encourage him not to drown his sorrows in alcohol, which can depress the mood and liquidate his asset. Interesting statistics for him to chew on: our brains are made up of around 75% water, our body weight is around 65–70% water and we lose up to 3 litres a day just in breath, sweat, tears and excretion. It helps keep the skin plump and staves off hunger pangs. We need to keep supplies replenished. We need water to survive. The way to go is H_2O.

Good fats and gangster fats

Fats can be smart and fats can be dumb, just like men (and women sometimes). Strangely enough, the 'uns' are the clever ones. Monounsaturated fats are the nice guys in town. Found in olive oil, fish, seafood and avocados, for example, they help provide the good cholesterol we need. Polyunsaturated (sounds like a girlfriend who doesn't like alcohol) fats help keep blood pressure and cholesterol levels down and are found in vegetable oils and oily fish. Saturated fats raise cholesterol levels and are found in animal fats, red meat, many dairy products and bacon. Your guy may need to go easy on these. The Gangster Fats are trans fats or hydrogenated, biochemically altered fats, recognised by the words hydrogenised or partially hydrogenised on the label. They may affect both brain function and general health and in excess can be very bad for us. Encourage him to box clever with his fat and his fats or they could box him back.

Mind his lunchbox

The benefits of a healthy mind-enhancing breakfast can be ruined by a fat-laden carb-fest pizza-based or burger-bound take-out lunch, with a beer to go ma'am. Oily fish is an excellent brain food – one or two portions a week of salmon, sardines, tuna, trout or herring (go easy on the rollmops in the office) will help provide a good supply of fatty acid omega-3, which helps the brain perform at its optimum level whatever our age. A deficiency is linked with mood swings, depression and poor memory. If you feel like making his lunch for him, a tuna salad with low-fat mayo or a smoked salmon sandwich on wholegrain bread would be a good choice. Meet him for lunch and go to a sushi bar – it's a delicious and healthy option. Mind his mind if he forgets to do it for himself.

Naked dining

A man's mood may lift voluntarily at the sound of cooking and eating naked in the evening. Food is great naked – whether he is may be another matter. Steaming vegetables and fish is good, grilling poultry and meat is better than frying, except in a low-fat stir-fry. Bin the batter, skim the skin, stuff the stuffing, move over Mayo, hello Olive Oil. Go for fresh, seasonal and organic (if possible) produce as much as both time and budget will allow. Grilled skinless chicken atop a mound of salad or poached salmon flanked by an array of interesting vegetables – mouth-watering but not waist-plumping. Try not to eat too late – some diets say no carbs after sundown – and ease up on the alcohol. You will both feel so much better the next day. Healthy body, healthy mind. What you drink should make you think not sink. Alcohol is a depressive. That is the last word on the subject.

What is he Really Thinking?

We have established that men and women communicate for different reasons and in different ways. You may well be under the impression on occasion that your guy is talking another language entirely. Does he mean what he says? Does he say what he means? Do you sometimes feel you need a simultaneous interpreter or a glossary in order to get the real message. If it's true that women use both sides of their brain when talking, then words (left hemisphere) will be connected to emotions (right hemisphere). If men just use one side, then language and feeling may well not be linked. If you have got half a mind to understand, read on. It might help you negotiate your way through the minefield of manspeak.

Context	He says	He's thinking
First encounter (in the street)	Excuse me, do you have the time?	Nice cleavage
First encounter (in the street)	Can I help you with that?	Nice body
First encounter (in the street)	Are you new around here?	Fresh meat, great!
First encounter (at a party)	Haven't we met before?	You look sexy
First encounter (at a party)	I just had to come and speak to you	I wonder what you look like naked
First encounter (at a party)	Are you busy at the weekend?	How much competition is there?
First encounter (at a party)	You're the most attractive woman here	I wonder if you still would be without clothes
First encounter (at a party)	Can I buy you a drink?	I'd like to take you home
First encounter (at a party)	Don't you think it's noisy in here?	Let's go outside and get to first base
First encounter (at a party)	Shall we go somewhere quiet?	I'll pay for the taxi back to my place
First encounter (at a party)	Can I have your mobile number?	I might just call, you lucky girl
First encounter (at a party)	Would you like to go to a movie sometime?	And go home and get to second base
First encounter (at a party)	I drive a sportscar	I've got an old banger with a big engine
First date	What would you like to do tonight?	I haven't bothered to plan anything
First date	Fancy a film?	Fancy a smooch on the back row?
First date	I am not really into musicals	Do I look gay?
First date	Let's just go for a romantic walk	I won't have to pay anything – result!

Context	He says	He's thinking
First date	I will call you	I probably won't, but I don't want to hurt you
First date	See you around	Goodbye
First date	Let's just have fun together	This is just a one-night stand
Second date	Dinner's on me	Chicken nuggets or burger?
Second date	I like the new hairstyle	Why did you cut all your hair off?
Second date	I'd like to see more of you	I would like to sleep with you
Second date	I think I could be falling in love with you	Let's sleep together soon
Second date	I think I love you	Let's have sex now
Second date	How many guys have you been with?	I am the best though, aren't I?
Third date	You remind me so much of my sister	This is going nowhere
Third date	I've only got eyes for you	I spotted that attractive girl
Third date	I think we are getting too serious	I've got my eye on a new babe
Third date	I need some space	I may dump you if the other babe says yes
Third date	I don't know what I want	I think I want the other babe
Third date	I'm just not good with words	I don't want to talk about the other babe
Later	Let's get married	No other guy is going to get you
Much later	I was listening to every word you said	I have no idea what you just said
Much later	Of course your bum doesn't look big	I'm too scared to say it's huge
Much later	I love you just the way you are	What happened to your butt?
Much later	That is the perfect dress	I'm leaving the shop now
Much later	I've got you a present	It was free with vouchers
Much later	Of course I missed you	Why did you come back so soon?
Much later	I know exactly where we are	We're lost but I'm not getting the map out

How to Handle Your Man and His Tools

Men don't like to admit inadequacy, defeat or failure. High on many men's list of things they may feel they cannot confess to disliking or not excelling at is DIY. Three little, apparently harmless letters represent an entire alphabet of grief. Is your man a DIY-king or DIY-impostor? DIY may begin as *'Do It? Yes!'* but end in *'Do It Yourself (if you're so great…)'*

The Bigger the Better (or Worse)

D I D
I T
Y E S T E R D A Y

D E F E R
I T
Y E A R L Y

D O
I T ?
Y E S   (in my own time)

D O
I T
Y O U R S E L F
(then, if you can do a better job…)

D O N ' T
I N T E R F E R E ,
Y O U !

D E T E S T
I T ?
Y E S !

The more buttons and knobs a tool has the better as far as a man is concerned. How many remote controls does your guy have?

Big tools

The only bit about DIY that some men really do like is the search for the biggest, latest, most powerful, all-singing, all-dancing, envy-inspiring tool. For some males, a drill is an indoor version of a low-slung sports car with all the extras, except perhaps the go-faster stripes. When selecting a utensil or machine, men can be seen strutting into the hardware showroom and spending hours hunting for the most streamline, turbo-charged one. Its instruction manual stays safely in the box, snuggling up with the guarantee. If they could take their tools with them to the club or bar, they would use them to attract the fairer sex, like their ancestors taking their latest axe to the Cave Idol competition.

Fiddle while Rome floods

Men like fiddling with electronics, computer software, electric train sets and remote-controlled toys, but fixing a dripping tap, sorting out a leaking lavatory or mending the cat flap are much less welcome tasks. It's similar with housework. Men's brains appear to be programmed not to see mess and dust. Their spatial skills don't account for this detail, apparently. A possible solution to this problem is to encourage your man to see how much more out of ten he would score (with emphasis on the verb) if he were to do his share of the household duties. Explain how much more time you would have to spend alone together in the bedroom if he did a spot of vacuuming and dusting in the living room first. He could lose around 200 calories with an hour of moderate activity downstairs and a few more upstairs later on...

Go buy the book

Buy a good home repair book for yourself and leave it lying around the place, open at a particularly relevant page. Get a mate of his to suggest they go to an evening class in plumbing – friends who drain together remain together, after all. If all else fails, join a course yourself, but don't tell him about the handsome tutors. Find a handsome plumber and keep the number to yourself. Don't share it with your girlfriends or all the benefit could go down the drain.

Men and gadgets

Men love the latest, the best, the most complicated gadgets that they can get their overexcited little hands on. If the vacuum cleaner had GPS they would use it more. One thing you'll notice is that no man will read an instruction manual; they think they were written by men for girls. However, you can always get him to read it by pretending not to understand it yourself.

Talking Him Round

There are things you should not say to a man trying to get a handle on DIY and others that will help things run as smoothly as a chainsaw through meringue.

YOU DON'T SAY:
- IT'S EXACTLY ONE YEAR TO THE DAY SINCE YOU STARTED TO FIX THAT CUPBOARD

- ARE YOU ABSOLUTELY SURE YOU KNOW WHAT YOU'RE DOING?

- IS THAT REALLY MEANT TO HAPPEN?

- NOW YOU HAVE TAKEN IT APART, ARE YOU GOING TO PUT IT BACK TOGETHER?

- WOULDN'T IT BE CHEAPER TO GET A PROFESSIONAL TO DO IT?

- I COULD HAVE DONE IT BETTER MYSELF

- JANE'S HUSBAND DOES ALL THEIR DIY JOBS. HE IS SO CLEVER

- WHY DON'T YOU ADMIT YOU ARE JUST NOT PRACTICAL?

- SHALL I JUST CALL DAD AND GET HIM TO FIX IT?

- I KNEW I SHOULD NEVER HAVE ASKED YOU TO DO IT

YOU DO SAY:
- LET'S RUN IT BY A PROFESSIONAL AND THEN I AM SURE YOU WILL KNOW EXACTLY WHAT TO DO

- YOU ARE TOO BUSY AND IMPORTANT TO BOTHER WITH SILLY LITTLE REPAIRS

- YOU LOOK SO SEXY IN YOUR OVERALLS

- WHAT A BIG DRILL YOU'VE GOT!

- MY GIRLFRIENDS WILL BE SO JEALOUS WHEN I TELL THEM

- I WILL LEAVE YOU ALONE FOR AN HOUR SO YOU CAN GET ON WITH IT

- SHALL I MAKE YOU A COFFEE WHILE YOU ARE DOING THAT, DARLING?

- I LOVE MEN IN UNIFORM

- WHY NOT LET THE PLUMBER FIX IT WHILE WE GO AWAY FOR THE WEEKEND SOMEWHERE ROMANTIC WITHOUT THE KIDS

- I HEAR THE PLUMBING EVENING CLASSES ARE FULL OF YOUNG WOMEN NOWADAYS

How to Help Men Score at the Store

Many men hate shopping, although a few actually enjoy cruising the stores. It might be difficult to believe, but research has shown that men make better shoppers than women. It's all to do with emotion. If a man is asked to buy the groceries, he will see it as an exercise – not quite a military one, but not far off. The enemy is the supermarket or store, the task the specific list of items required and the reward, its consumption, a few brownie points or a bit of time in the 'man-bubble.' It was much more straightforward when the choice was freshly killed burger or raw fish with low-calorie entrails.

He's a Smooth Shoperator

It all goes back to the cave. Mrs Cavewoman would ask her man to go out and get dinner from the 'so fresh you can hear it breathing' counter at the open-air market. The mission was clear, the motive survival. Mr Caveman came back, mission accomplished and feeling good. We are more searcher-shoppers than hunter-gatherers nowadays, but the principle is much the same. The process is rather less gruesome and physically taxing, but it's still a cut-throat world out there.

For many women shopping is a way of relaxing, of making themselves feel better, of stimulating those feel-good hormones. For men it is rarely any of those things, but men stray less from the grocery list and are less likely to buy on impulse than women. Men shop with intent, which is why they find it somewhat exasperating to sit outside a changing room while their partner deliberates for several hours over what looks like a bewildering array of identical outfits (at least, that's how it may seem to him). Try not to put your man through this experience too often. Take a girlfriend instead. If he is treating you to a new outfit, find the one you want on a first shopping expedition and then take him back for the parade and purchase, or just straight purchase.

If you want to encourage your man to score at the store, give him a list, with as many details about size, brand, price and so on as possible. Leave as little room for doubt as you can. You could even give him a visual list, with labels from previous purchases attached or scanned in and boxes for him to tick. Being unspecific is like issuing him with orders to invade one country, but telling him that the one next door will do just fine. Encourage the hunter-shopper. Tell him he has done a great job. Don't turn him into a basket case. Use your loyalty card and reward him – put 'Buy yourself a bar of chocolate' at the end of the list. No need to specify which one in this case. Tell him he looks sexy with a trolley and drives it better than any Formula One driver would.

Getting what you want

If your man is not good at remembering birthdays, Valentine's Day and anniversaries or at buying gifts for those special occasions, you will have to help him out if you are to get what you want. Drop subtle but noticeable hints about at impending date, but don't do it while he is watching a match on television or underneath the car. 'Jackie's guy bought her a great gift for Valentine's Day last year', 'I can't believe it's my birthday again soon' or 'I would love to go to that restaurant for our anniversary' might work. More overt tactics would include writing in his diary, emailing him a list of forthcoming events or putting a picture of your ideal gift on the refrigerator or the windscreen of his car. Drawing a picture of it in lipstick on the bathroom mirror is a step too far. A note on the underside of the toilet seat is an option.

Giving him what he wants

Relationships are all about give and take. Think of your partnership as an equation. If you each give 50% you'll get 100%, but it could be so much better. Double your efforts and you get twice as much out of it. Your man could do the maths in his head of course, but it would look like this: 50% + 50% = 100% but 100% + 100% = 200%. Ask him what he would really like from you. You could each draw up a 'wish list' and swop. You may find that just spending some relaxing 'quality' time together is the best gift. Being present can be a present in itself. Small gestures are often the most appreciated.

Beware his tactics

Men will often pretend not to know how to do things or will do them so badly that you don't ask them to do it again. This applies to most chores: washing up, vacuuming, dusting, shopping, changing nappies, ironing and so on.

Men think that an overblown gesture makes up for a lack of help or consideration. He gives you a huge bunch of flowers and thinks the problem is sorted. Don't fall for it. Tell him that an apology and a bit of effort is worth much more.

You Don't Say

- JUST BUY THE THINGS YOU THINK WE NEED
- YOU PLAN THE MEALS FOR THIS WEEK AND BUY ALL THE INGREDIENTS
- WHY ON EARTH DID YOU BUY THAT?
- ANY OLD BRAND, ANY OLD SIZE, ANY OLD FLAVOUR

You Do Say

- HERE'S A LIST OF EVERYTHING WE NEED, ARRANGED BY AISLE, WITH SIZES AND BRANDS MARKED
- LET'S GO SHOPPING TOGETHER AND GET SOME THINGS YOU REALLY LIKE
- IF YOU DO THE SHOPPING, I WILL COOK US A ROMANTIC, CANDLE-LIT MEAL
- THERE'S A MODEL WORKING PART-TIME IN THE MALL
- IF YOU COULD TRY TO REMEMBER TO LOOK AT THE SELL-BY DATES THAT WOULD BE GREAT

Love & Friendship

In or Out?
When women kiss they tend to stick their bottoms out. When men kiss, they stick their bottoms in.

Holding Hands
Holding hands indicates equal status in a relationship. Nobody has the upper hand and both partners accept each other on an equal footing.

A Good Sign
First our parents, then our lovers and then our children hold our hands. It is a gesture of support, trust, intimacy and protection.

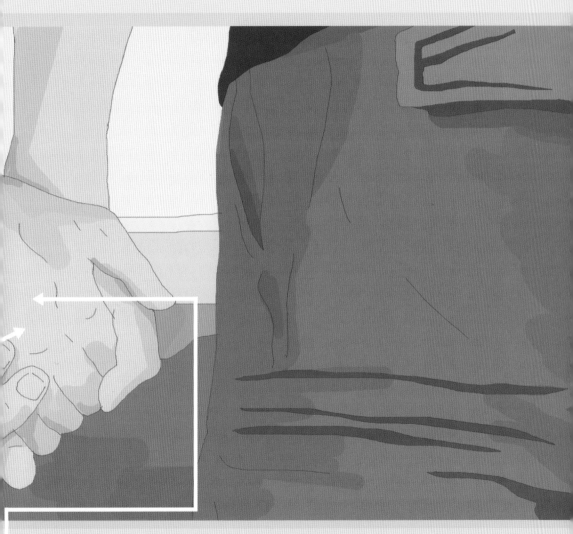

'Like mouth to mouth resuscitation, a spot of heart to heart can revive a relationship by injecting it with fresh oxygen. They go hand in hand.'
JOANNA RAMPLEY-STURGEON, 2004

Touchy Feely
Physical contact of this type is important. It raises levels of the 'cuddle hormone', oxytocin, which makes women more sexually receptive and likely to bond with their partner.

What is Love Really all About?

Now let's turn to that really big, universal, makes-the-world-go-round, turns-it-upside-down emotion. Amour, amore, love – there are so many ways to say it. What is love? What's it all about? What happens when you fall in love? How do you know if a man really loves you? What is the difference between body-love and mind-love? These questions have preoccupied scientists, anthropologists, novelists, agony aunts and Master, Mr, Ms and Mrs Human for centuries. Nobody really knows the full answer – love is an elusive and often fragile thing. Read on to find out more.

WHAT IS LOVE?

L O V E
O B L I T E R A T E S
V I R T U A L L Y
E V E R Y T H I N G

It seems that the powerful hormonal rush that occurs when we fall in love makes us, quite literally, blind to any faults our love object may have. We overlook any negative aspects (for example, a lack of height, hair, hard pecs, humour or handsome features) and see both the love object and our joint future through seriously rose-tinted spectacles (do note that it is the same for men and women). Love is a drug, a brain potion, a heady cocktail of neurotransmitters and chemicals with more than a dash of testosterone and oestrogen, shaken, stirred and put in a blender. One good gulp and men and women are soon blind drunk and heading to horizontal harmony. Shakespeare was right all along. An ugly Bottom can get our Titania-breasts beating wildly.

Lust (let's call it body-love) may well play a key role in the first phase of a romance, particularly for a man. All that testosterone swirling around is bound to have an effect. This is a whirlwind phase, full of passion as the potion takes effect and the pheromones (airborne chemicals) are really doing their stuff. Watch out, girls, just a whiff of the pheromones and we go weak at the knees. More about whiffs later (see page 72).

Researchers have discovered that a pesky little substance called phenylethylamine (PEA for short) is the love-drug, the cupid or the culprit, depending on how things turn out. Remember that lovely, warm feeling when you were literally floating on air? You were floating on PEA. Sounds much less romantic. You could pretend it stands for Pleasantly Erotic Aroma – his and yours.

If you were to look at the brain of someone in love, it would not look hugely different from the brain of a chef who got magic mushrooms confused with shitake and tasted his own dish. It's addictive stuff and slightly hallucinogenic. Love certainly makes the world go round, and round, and round... and some of us get dizzy and others are actually ill. We can all get addicted to love, but sometimes we wake up too early or too late and an emotional hangover is our only reward. Other more successful partnerships develop and deepen and the partners bond and become deeply attached as they prepare to become a family. The volatile, volcanic feelings settle down into much more manageable and predictable emotions. Some guys can't handle this plateau stage and need new excitement. Watch out for those if you are looking for long-term love. He won't like the 'C' words such as comfy, commitment, companionship, compromise...

But how do you tell if your chosen one is consumed by lust or infused with love? Eyes right if you would like to check out some of the signs to look out for. Take the test yourself, too. You might be surprised by the results. Anything over 60% ain't bad, as the song goes...

PERFECT PETER

Perfect Peter will score highly in this questionnaire. Give him some brownie points if he does.

A Different Kind of Questionnaire:

Check out the following signs of lust turning to love. Each one gets a point:

1. CLAMMY HANDS (NICER AND LESS MOIST THAN SIMPLY SWEATY ONES)

2. FLUSHED CHEEKS (THINK RED RIDING HOOD WITH STUBBLE TROUBLE)

3. RACING HEART (FEEL IT, SKIN ON SKIN IS BEST – DON'T JUST TAKE HIS WORD FOR IT)

4. SLIGHTLY IRRATIONAL BEHAVIOUR (A DIFFERENT KIND OF IRRATIONAL FROM USUAL)

5. CRAZY ROMANTIC GESTURES (WEEKENDS AWAY, FLOWERS, CHOCOLATES, HOT-AIR BALLOON TRIPS, ABSEILING VOUCHERS)

6. LOSS OF APPETITE (NOT JUST DUE TO A DIET OR HANGOVER; REAL, NOTICEABLE, TROUSER-LOOSENING WEIGHT LOSS)

7. BUILD UP OF MUSCLE (REGULAR VISITS TO GYM TO DOUBLE HIS THREE-PACK)

8. SIGNS OF AN OBSESSIVE TENDENCY (CAN'T STOP CALLING, EMAILING, TEXTING)

9. CAN'T BEAR TO BE APART FROM YOU FOR A MINUTE (THIS CAN GET CLAUSTROPHOBIC AND LOSE ITS APPEAL)

10. SHOWERS YOU WITH DIAMONDS, GOLD, FAKE FUR AND... (ADD YOUR HEARTFELT DESIRE HERE IN CASE HE READS THIS BIT)

11. MAKES CONSTANT EYE CONTACT WHEN YOU ARE WITH HIM (WATCH OUT WHEN CROSSING ROADS)

12. CAN'T STOP HOLDING HANDS OR TOUCHING YOUR FACE (TRICKY WHEN YOU GO TO THE BATHROOM)

13. SAYS YOU LOOK EVEN MORE BEAUTIFUL WITHOUT MAKE-UP

14. STARTS WEARING THE SAME STYLE AND COLOUR CLOTHES AS YOU

15. SAYS HE LOVES YOUR ZITS

16. SERENADES YOU FROM THE STREET AT MIDNIGHT (YOU LIVE ON THE 10TH FLOOR)

17. BRISTLES VISIBLY IF ANOTHER MALE MAKES ADVANCES (EVEN IF IT IS THE WAITER ASKING FOR YOUR ORDER)

18. INTRODUCES YOU TO ALL HIS FRIENDS AS 'MY GIRLFRIEND/PARTNER' (SWEET)

19. INTRODUCES YOU TO HIS PARENTS (SCARY BUT SWEET)

20. INTRODUCES YOU TO HIS BOSS (TERRIFYING)

21. INTRODUCES YOU TO HIS BANK ACCOUNT (LESS TERRIFYING)

22. SAYS 'WE' A LOT OR 'MY OTHER HALF' (SWEET BUT NAUSEATING FOR SOME)

23. GIVES YOU THE KEY TO HIS FLAT

24. GIVES YOU THE KEY TO HIS CAR

25. TELLS YOU HIS LAPTOP PASSWORD

26. GIVES YOU HIS CREDIT CARD

It's Amore

If your guy is a man of few words, remind him that humans have a total vocabulary of around 60,000 words. In reality, of course, we only need a fraction of this number to get by on a day-to-day basis – but there's no need to tell him that. In this section, we're interested in just three words. They're not complicated, but they can mean so much and speak volumes – and be with you for ever and ever.

I Love You

I LOVE YOU = I fancy you big time

I LOVE YOU = ...but I can't remember your name

I LOVE YOU = Let's go upstairs

I LOVE YOU = ...and tomorrow I'm going to try and get you upstairs

I LOVE YOU = If I don't say this, we will never go upstairs

I LOVE YOU = I think I am meant to say I love you

I LOVE YOU = I don't think I do but I think I should

I LOVE YOU = I love you and I love my other girlfriend and I love that girl in the pub...

I LOVE YOU = I want to spend the immediate future with you

I LOVE YOU = I want to go on holiday with you

I LOVE YOU = ...almost as much as I love my dog

I LOVE YOU = ...when you do that to me

I LOVE YOU = ...when you have no clothes on

I LOVE YOU = ...when you wear that underwear I bought you

I LOVE YOU = ...when you are quiet

I LOVE YOU = ...when you don't nag me

I LOVE YOU = ...when you don't try to change me

I LOVE YOU = ...when you don't wear those huge knickers

I LOVE YOU = ...when you cook a Sunday roast for me

I LOVE YOU = ...when you don't care if I vomit on your sofa

I LOVE YOU = ...when you don't ask me to clear it up

I LOVE YOU = ...when you don't tell my mum I am completely drunk

I LOVE YOU = ...when you let me be a sofa slob with all the remotes

I LOVE YOU = I care about you

I LOVE YOU = I want you around

I LOVE YOU = I really do love you

I LOVE YOU = I think I love you

I LOVE YOU = I want to spend the rest of my life with you

I LOVE YOU = I love the way I feel around you

I LOVE YOU = ...and respect you and want to cherish you

I Love You all Around the World

CANTONESE CHINESE

Ngo oiy ney a

DUTCH

Ik hou van jou

FRENCH

Je t'aime, Je t'adore

GERMAN

Ich liebe dich

GREEK

S'agapo

HINDI

Hum Tumhe Pyar Karte hae

ITALIAN

Ti amo

JAPANESE

Aishiteru

MANDARIN CHINESE

Wo ai ni

MOROCCAN

Ana moajaba bik

PORTUGUESE

Eu te amo

RUSSIAN

Ya tebya liubliu

SPANISH

Te quiero / Te amo

SWEDISH

Jag alskar dig

WELSH

'Rwy'n dy garu di

YIDDISH

Ikh hob dikh

Now You're Talking, Love

Love has the power to send us to delirious, heady heights of happiness, but it can also dump us into depths of dark despair if it all goes wrong. Love rarely runs smoothly – it is a rollercoaster, a big dipper, a merry-go-round, a terrifying ride that makes our tummies churn. And then there's the ghost train when it becomes history. Just try to avoid having any skeletons in your closet.

Love Has the Power

Love is a bond that holds you and your partner together and with it you can face difficulties and remain partners. Establishing that bond and the trust that goes with it involves lots of 'C' words: compromise, co-operation, commitment, common interests and, above all, communication.

In the A–Z of Love men prefer to turn straight to the page marked 'S'. 'C' is not usually a well-thumbed page. Leave the book open at 'C' (metaphorically speaking) or if 'S', then at the entry for support. However, remember to erase the entry under 'C' for Changing Your Man. Don't make it obvious that change is on the cards and on your mind.

Love Letters

Why not commit your feelings to paper and write a love letter or poem to your partner? It can be easier than saying it out loud sometimes. Tell him all the things you really love about who he is, what he does, how he supports you. Tell him how romantic you find his gestures, how much you appreciate and value him, the ways he makes you feel special.

Pop it in his briefcase before he goes to work or in his suitcase before he goes on a business trip. Don't email it to his office and copy all your friends in or send to a poetry competition.

Express Yourself

Love is a powerful thing. It has started wars, it has ended films, it has inspired songwriters, composers, artists, sculptors, novelists, poets, dramatists, film makers, fashion designers, chocolatiers, chefs and entire movements. Where would we be without love?

Writing about love and its ups and downs is not just for professionals. The very act of writing down how you feel can be very therapeutic and can dispel some feelings of frustration, annoyance or downright anger. Why not give it a go?

The Written Word

When something is worrying or distressing you, why not write it down in a journal first and get rid of some of the anger or disappointment. Pinpoint the issues and even suggest possible solutions – things you or your partner can do to make life better or easier. Then you can set aside some time to discuss them.

Don't impose your solutions, raise them as potential but not final answers, maybe after he has suggested some of his own. Allow him to come up with his way of fixing things. Men like to be Mr Fix-Its, even when the problem is an emotional one.

The Love Alphabet

In the ABC of Love, A is for accepting him. B is for believing in him. C is for comprehending and sometimes congratulating him. D is for devoting enough time to your relationship. E is for encouraging and educating him about what you need from the partnership. Let's stop at F.

In the Not ABC of Love, A is not for altering or annihilating him. B is not for badgering endlessly or belittling in public. C is not for changing him completely. D is not for destroying him. E is not for expecting him to change. You can take over now. X will be a challenge.

Let Love do the Talking

Love can be rocky. The road to romance can sometimes be dug up unexpectedly and repairs can require time and manpower. Traffic may be stopped in both directions for a while, emotional journeys and encounters postponed, suspended or cancelled. Patience and communication are needed. Heart, brain, mouth is the order of the day. Not mouth, heart, brain – that way chaos lies.

Being a good listener is a great skill to have. It is important to maintain eye contact with the speaker, give encouraging nods of the head or make the odd 'mmmm' sound and rest your chin on your hand if you are both seated. Let him have the platform. Your turn will come.

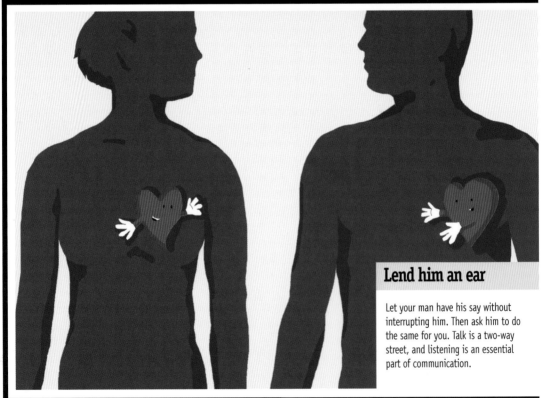

Heart to Heart

Lend him an ear

Let your man have his say without interrupting him. Then ask him to do the same for you. Talk is a two-way street, and listening is an essential part of communication.

✔ Do-Do's

All the following activities could seriously improve your relationship:

1. Be all ears

Listen, really listen, to what a man is saying. Use all your hearing and thinking capacity – both ears, all your brain and lots of patience. Half-a-brain listening is their talent. Yours is to lend an ear and shoulder so lend all – be generous. Hear every word and hang on to it.

Show him you are interested and concerned. He is on stage, you are in the stalls and no heckling is allowed or you will be shown the door. Don't get your knitting out or do the washing up while he is talking.

2. Be direct

When you explain your feelings and concerns about your relationship, be direct but not confrontational. Word games don't work. Save them for the crossword or charades at Christmas. Say what you have to say as honestly, calmly and directly as you can without

being aggressive, without apportioning blame and without sounding as if you are trying to change him. It is not a lecture but a conversation. If a man thinks you are trying to change him, he will respond with fright or flight tactics.

3. Hold back

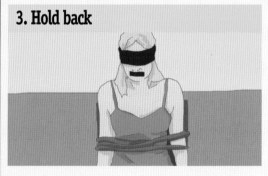

Go easy on your man. You may feel like wounding him verbally, if not actually punching him on the nose, but try to contain your anger and show tact and compassion (uh oh another 'C' word). He probably needs you to enlighten him about your feelings, so starting with a

missile attack will not solve anything. It may destroy his willingness to discuss anything further, along with his will to live. Remember: he is not a mind reader. Don't shed fake tears – men can't handle it when women cry. Keep it real.

4. Sleep well

Resolve the issue before you go to sleep. It is fine to sleep on a decision but don't turn the lights out on an argument. It will still be there in the morning and resentment may have grown overnight. Emotional vampires could come out in the dark and suck

understanding, compromise and reason out of both of you, leaving you without the resources needed to settle a dispute or talk rationally about it. Let the sun go down on a row at your peril, or at least tie some garlic to the bedpost.

Don't Make a Song and Dance

Love is like ballroom dancing. The band is playing a slow dance and the girl wants to smooch with her man, but he is showing off his tango talents and making dramatic movements. It takes two to tango, as the saying says, and one of you may be out of step. Don't make it worse or you will fall flat on your face. Read on for how to dance in tandem and stay in tune with your partner. Take it step by step and you won't face the music afterwards.

If he doesn't want to dance or talk, let him be for a while. He may not like the song or it may bring back bad memories. Perhaps he tripped up last time he tried. Put your name on his dance card for later.

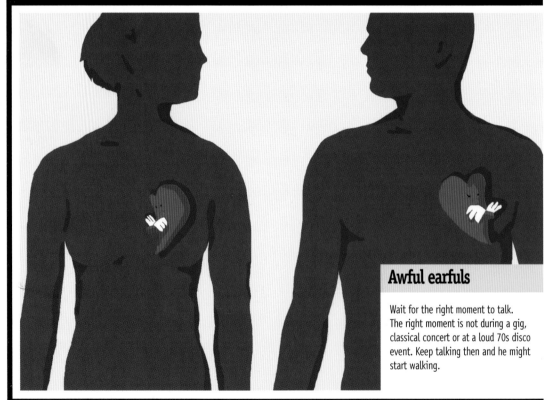

Don't Talk the Walk

Awful earfuls

Wait for the right moment to talk. The right moment is not during a gig, classical concert or at a loud 70s disco event. Keep talking then and he might start walking.

✖ No-No's

All of the following could seriously damage your relationship:

1. Don't be a know-it-all

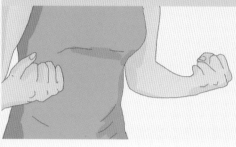

Don't interrupt when a man is trying to explain what is worrying him, even if he seems to be struggling to do so. Don't assume you know the whole story. Give him space and time to express his concerns. Don't keep saying 'I know what you are going to say' because a) you may not and b) it is going to irritate him, big time. Encourage him with non-verbal support signals like nods of the head or sympathetic looks. Clenching fists, tapping feet and pursing lips are not support signals.

2. Do not go past

Don't continually rake up the past, however great the temptation to do so or overwhelming the sense of justification. Imagine you are at a crossroads. One arrow says Back to the Past (bumpy route, 10 miles), the other To the Future (new surface, 5 miles). Try to visualise the future and work out how you can move forward successfully and together. Looking over your shoulder all the time will only cause crashes.

3. Don't use minus signs

Try not to criticise and blame him too much. Positive reinforcement works better than negative judgement. Too much emphasis on what a man has done wrong will simply provoke a fight or fright response. In an attempt to defend himself against your apparent attack, he may launch a few verbal stones from his sling before retreating into his 'man-bubble.' Constructive conversation is much more successful. Add it to the list of 'C' words.

4. Don't lock him out

Don't expect men to be mind readers with supernatural psychic powers. They don't come with crystal balls. You're probably not a mind reader either, but keep this to yourself. Men do not know what is going on in your head unless you tell them. They tend to be more transparent than women, and whereas most women can read men like a book, most men find women as impenetrable as locked treasure chests without keys. You have to hand them a key and show them the lock.

The Way to a Man's Heart is Via the Nose

What are noses for? It is pretty obvious why we need to see, hear, touch and taste our guys but why do we need to smell them? Some men might actually be more attractive if we were unable to inhale their body odour. Who knows what our noses do in a relationship. Read on…

Those Pesky Pheromones

Love may well lead us by the nose, but in fact it is through our nostrils that we are attracted to potential mates. Understanding sexual attraction relies on a sixth sense and a special scent. Heaven scent perhaps. We are talking pheromones again – subtle odours that each person emits. It is more a case of love at first sniff than love at first sight. Noses across a crowded room – it's quite an image. Perhaps that is why love is described as being 'in the air', floating around like pollen looking for a bee.

Smell gets to the brain amazingly quickly. It fast-forwards itself to the brain's emotional centre in record time. That is why it is such a powerful sense and one that can prompt powerful emotional memories.

Mr Dissimilar

It seems that we are all looking for someone with a different genetic make-up to our own, and one way of detecting Mr or Miss Right is to sniff them out. If we all procreated with The Similar One rather than The Dissimilar One, the gene pool would be for paddling rather than for Olympic lengths. Too much cologne or perfume and we may not find each other. A heavy cold and we probably won't either. Don't share this information with your guy if he is already a one-shower-a-week man.

It's a question of a delicate balance between washing regularly and still emitting our natural body scent. Just look how dogs greet each other with a sniff – no need to start at the wrong end like they do…

A Smell to Remember

Imagine talking to a friend about how you fell in love with your guy. 'Just one whiff and I knew he was the one for me' sounds a little unusual, but it happens. Smells can invoke some pretty strong emotional responses – whether or not you realise it at the time. Remember how as a child you used to love your teddy, blanket or whatever so much because of the comforting smell he/she/it had? Men can be like that. And they like to spend lots of time on your pillow, too.

It's Good to be Sniffy

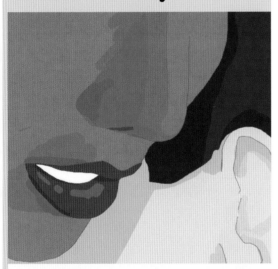

Try sniffing your friends, potential and existing lovers, even your dog. Your 'exes' may not appreciate you calling to check out their whiff, just so you can reassure yourself they were not The One after all. Ask first if it is OK for you to act like a puppy and snuffle around their hairline. Don't slobber and do limit yourself to this zone or the wrist. Lower is for later. It's a fascinating exercise, rather like taking part in an exotic wine tasting. You could end up just as heady and weak-kneed or simply pass out.

If male scent was bottled it could sell for millions on the world market. Imagine being able to buy Eau de James Bond? Chocolates and perfume would be all a girl needed.

Be Sniffy not Whiffy

Personal hygiene (his more than yours presumably) should not be sacrificed on the altar of animal magnetism. Body odour, like excessive cologne, could mask the true scent of someone or discourage its discovery. Think of the lovely smell of new babies' bottoms and how it makes us feel – warm all over and all nurturing. You wouldn't feel the same if it was covered in aftershave. So don't bathe in perfume. A light sprinkling in key areas (wrists and back of neck) and let your own heaven scent send him into seventh heaven.

As with most things, subtlety is the answer. Keep him guessing and sniffing. See if he has the bottle to chat you up.

Heart Savvy

Question: what is about the size of an orange, weighs no more than a bag of flour and works 24/7/365 – just to keep your guy alive? Answer: the heart. In the 4th century BC, Aristotle, the Greek philosopher, identified the heart as the seat of intelligence, motion and sensation. He thought it had three chambers and that the other organs existed just to keep it cool. It was William Harvey, physician to King Charles I, who many centuries later discovered the role it plays in the circulation of blood. He wasn't quite King of Hearts but doctor to him at least. The heart pumps five litres of blood per minute. It's some machine. Respect...

Hale and Hearty

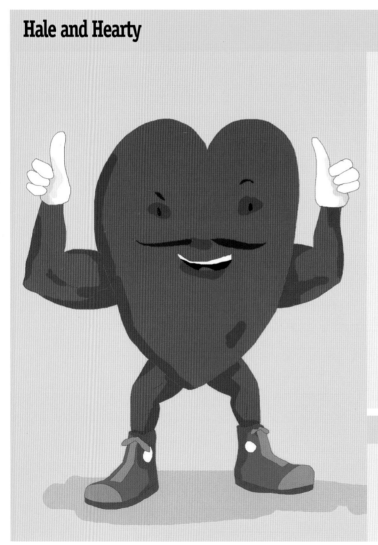

DID YOU KNOW?

- The heart is a muscle that needs to be flexed just like any other muscle.

- Your man should consult your doctor before going from zero to hero on the exercise front, and so should you.

- Green and black tea both contain polyphenols, the antioxidant properties of which can act as a defence against heart disease. Fancy a cuppa?

- Jogging is a very cheap sport that's great for your heart. There's no need to buy loads of costly equipment – good footwear is about all you require.

Chocolate: a healthy choice?

Research suggests that dark chocolate may be good for your heart (and not just in the sense of romance) - it contains antioxidants that increase 'good' cholesterol levels by as much as 10%.

A whole lotta lovin'

If you are lookin' for a whole lotta lovin' keep your man's heart strong and healthy. The best side effect of this is a whole lotta livin'. The heart is a muscle and needs flexing in order to grow stronger. Be queen of hearts by making sure he looks after his and then he can return the favour. Regular aerobic exercise will keep the heart working out and make it and him healthier. And he will burn lots of calories, too. Good result all round.

Hopping and skipping

Skipping indoors is a good aerobic exercise when time is short. The results might make your heart skip a beat next time he wears just a smile. When spring is springing and love is in the air, suggest you cycle into the countryside for a romantic picnic in a quiet, secluded field to study the birds and the bees. Brisk walking, jogging, swimming and aerobic classes are also good and gardening, dancing or walking the dog are also useful exercises, if not exactly aerobic. And going upstairs is also good for you...

The heart of the matter

Before leaping into an exercise programme, check with you doctor, particularly if there is any family or personal history of heart disease. Heart problems don't rule out exercise but you do need to check with a professional before embarking on a rigorous schedule of activities. Start gently – he doesn't need to go from couch potato to marathon trainer in one week. He'll be back to a 'fed-up with this malarkey' sofa slob in no time. Aim for 20–30 minutes at a time, say three times a week to start and then build it up.

Do the sums

Once the doctor has given the thumbs up, your man will need to monitor the intensity of his exercise. Men are good at maths so he may enjoy working out his target heart rate. For most healthy males, the target heart rate is between 50 and 75% of the maximum heart rate for their age. Your guy may need a calculator unless he scores well at percentages.

He should check his heart rate during and just after exercise. The best places to check the pulse are on the wrist at the base of the thumb (radial pulse) and the neck, just to the side of the Adam's apple (carotid pulse). Why not play nurse? Looking at your watch, count the number of beats in 15 seconds. Multiply by four to get the number of beats per minute (60 seconds). Say the heart beats 18 times in 15 seconds when he is sitting watching television, his resting heart rate or pulse is 72. You could buy your guy a heart-rate monitor if you are both better at anatomy than maths.

Blood pressure

High blood pressure (hypertension) is a key issue in men's health. Up to one in five Western men have high blood pressure. Don't let your guy become a statistic or remain blissfully unaware that he may become one. Regular blood pressure checks are vital – particularly as men get older. Those who have high blood pressure over a long period of time are more likely to suffer a heart attack, stroke or kidney failure.

Row the boat ashore

Rowing is possibly the best all-round exercise for both heart and body, so for his birthday you could buy him a rowing machine. You might enjoy it too. The motion is actually quite satisfying. Another way to push the boat out would be to treat your guy to a weekend away in a hotel boasting long walks by the sea and spas full of treatments as rewards later.

If you can't afford a weekend away, plan some nearby walks at the weekend. Regular brisk walks will help tone his muscles, lower his cholesterol levels, manage his body weight and strengthen his heart and cardiovascular system (thereby reducing the risk of heart attack). What's more, they help boost his immune system, self-esteem and energy levels while lifting his mood. A massage will get him in a different kind of mood. Result all round (well, less round than before in certain places...).

Work it Out

Subtract his age from 220 to get the maximum heart rate (MHR) and multiply that number by 0.5 and then 0.75. If your guy is 30 then his MHR will be 220 minus 30 = 190. 190 x 0.5 = 95 and 190 x 0.75 = 143. His target heart rate is somewhere between 95 and 143.

If you find he needs some improvement, what better way to a man's heart than via the latest technology? There are some ultra-modern, ultra-cool tools out there to monitor all types of exercise. How about a watch that comes with a heart-rate monitor and, even more exciting (for him, not you) a satellite tracking unit? Your guy can strap it to his body before training and then download the data to a PC and analyse the results. He will know where he stands in all senses. Oh yes, make sure he buys some proper trainers – wearing his old ones from school is not an option and flash doesn't always mean fleet of foot...

More Heart Savvy

As we all know, eating healthily has major health benefits. Not least, it can protect your man against heart disease. However, a good diet can have some other beneficial side effects... Try to get your guy to eat for his heart and then he might start singing for his supper. Serve him a healthy, romantic meal studded with aphrodisiacs, and see if he's stimulated enough to serenade you.

Food for Love

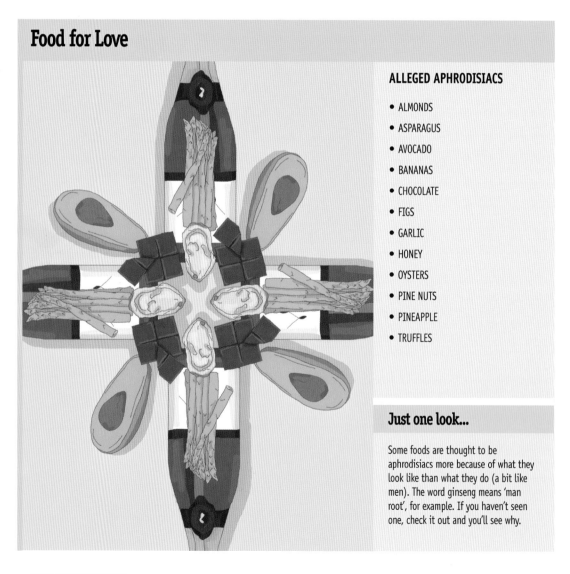

ALLEGED APHRODISIACS

- ALMONDS
- ASPARAGUS
- AVOCADO
- BANANAS
- CHOCOLATE
- FIGS
- GARLIC
- HONEY
- OYSTERS
- PINE NUTS
- PINEAPPLE
- TRUFFLES

Just one look...

Some foods are thought to be aphrodisiacs more because of what they look like than what they do (a bit like men). The word ginseng means 'man root', for example. If you haven't seen one, check it out and you'll see why.

Eat your heart into shape

Certain foods are particularly good for the heart. Let's start with the nuts and oats (no, not those or those...). Nuts are full of monounsaturated fats (the good fats, see page 53) and studies have shown that frequent consumption lowers the risk of heart disease by between 15 and 50%. Walnuts are a good source of omega-3 fats (like salmon) and these help to 'thin' the blood and prevent the formation of clots that can block blood vessels and cause heart attacks and strokes.

Nuts and oats

Almonds are an excellent source of antioxidant vitamin E, associated with a reduced risk of heart disease and cancer. Brazil nuts are a rich source of antioxidant selenium, a mineral linked to lower rates of heart disease and cancer. Avoid roasted nuts, since they are often deep fried in oil high in saturates. Dry-roasted nuts are a better choice. Go for unsalted ones, too. Oats are full of a type of soluble fibre called beta glucan, which can help lower blood cholesterol levels and the risk of heart disease and stroke. Getting his daily oats is good for him. It's official.

Popeye and Olive Oil

Garlic lowers cholesterol levels and thins the blood. It is better if you both eat it, as its powers are both protective and pungent. Go to bed wearing fangs and a black cloak and he might get the message (or he might quite like it...). Just the word broccoli fills some with gloom and thoughts of soggy stalks and flaccid florets, but it is delicious *al dente* and tasty raw. Packed with vitamins and minerals, it is a heart-friendly food. You and your guy could munch on it while watching a DVD. It beats a packet of crisps any day.

Olive oil is rich in monounsaturates, thought to help reduce the risk of heart disease by lowering gangster or LDL cholesterol and increasing good or HDL cholesterol. It is also linked with preventing wrinkles – when eaten rather than rubbed on the face. Omega-3 (present in oily fish, see page 53) helps prevent the formation of blood clots that can block blood vessels and cause a heart attack or stroke. Salmon, tuna and sardines are great suppliers of omega-3.

Berry good for you and get fruity

Blueberries are the Berry Idols of the fruit world – anti-ageing, antioxidant, anti-bad cholesterol and anti-high blood-pressure levels. Low in fat, they contain fibre – pretty much the all-rounder on the fruit team. Put them on the list (see page 23). Apples are thought to help keep cholesterol out of the blood – an apple a day keeps the heart doctor away. It supplies the flavonoid quercetin, an antioxidant that protects artery walls and helps your blood to flow smoothly. Grape juice has flavonoids too, but that doesn't mean you can drink wine in the same way!

Food for thought, food for love

If music be the food of love, play on, wrote the Bard. If aphrodisiacs be the food of love, eat your fill, and if oysters are the stuff of passion, munch on or just swallow. Mention aphrodisiacs and most people think of oysters. Casanova certainly did – he ate dozens a day to keep up his amorous momentum and stamina. There are lots of other alleged aphrodisiacs but none have been proved guilty beyond doubt in the laboratory or court of love yet. Oysters are indeed high in zinc, which plays a key role in the production of testosterone, so there may be a strong case for these little critters. They are also full of vitamins and thought to boost the metabolism, thereby battling the bulge (and possibly enhancing its performance...). Serve them as a starter, and desserts might be unexpectedly interesting.

Aztec love

The Aztecs called the avocado tree the ahuacuatl, or testicle tree (no guesses why). Avocado is good for the heart in that it helps lower blood cholesterol levels; it is bursting with a plant compound known as glutathione, linked with protection against heart disease. You could always mash one and make a mouth-watering spread. Asparagus has a certain visual quality that puts it in the aphrodisiac league. Feed your guy steamed asparagus for a sensuous culinary experience, tips dipped in olive oil. Ginger helps stimulate the circulatory system. Why not whip up a stir-fry with freshly grated ginger and invent your own fresh spice later.

Chocolate: love it and log it

Chocolate helps boost the feel-good factor in our grey cells, so finish off with some nice dark chocolate (60–70% cocoa) and see what conversation topics come up. Experiment at home and keep a log of results – but don't discuss it with your girlfriends until your guy is out of earshot. Good news for chocoholics, who may be delighted, if a little surprised, to discover that chocolate has antioxidant properties and is a good source of magnesium and iron. Some very nice dental experts have suggested it might protect teeth by coating them with cocoa butter. Other research has been done into its soothing properties – for the throat and the soul. It is thought to be more effective at soothing coughs than codeine. Isn't that the best news?

Iron man

If your guy is always tired, listless and down (in all senses) he may be anaemic and need some extra iron to become Popeye again (it might be worth checking with the doctor). A nice juicy steak might just get those muscles pumping. Don't forget to involve Olive Oil, if Popeye is in need. Speaking of which, spinach is high in folate and thought to reduce homocysteine, the compound linked to heart disease.

9 Ways to be Queen of His Heart

Relationships are like double mattresses – they need to breathe or they go stale. Let your relationship have some air. Actively encourage your man to spend time with his male friends or treat him to a day enjoying his favourite sport (without you). Don't pull a face or heave a deep sigh if he says he is going out for a potentially rowdy evening or stag weekend with the guys. Give it some oxygen and your relationship will stay fresh.

The Queen's Crown

Heart to heart

Remember how good you feel when he does something really nice for you? Think what you could do to make him feel wanted, appreciated, special, the focus of undivided attention – all the things you like. No need for an expensive, grand, over-the-top gesture, such as booking a table at the new restaurant in town where the food is below average and the prices beyond belief and over budget. Cook his favourite meal and enjoy a candle-lit evening with him at home (no commute to the sofa afterwards) and talk to each other in a relaxed atmosphere. Just the two of you.

Absence makes the heart grow fonder

If you hit an obstacle on the path to romance, park and take time out to think if you are heading to the same, or even the right, destination. Give each other some space and distance. If you pursue your man nose to tail, he may think there is a bunny boiler at the wheel. A chance to think about where you are heading helps you get there in the end. And taking a turn off the highway can leave him wondering where you are and who you are with and what you are doing...

Love the man he is

Men want to be appreciated and loved for the way they are and not the way they may become once a good woman gets her hands on them. They like the idea of being seen as fixers not fixable or, worse case scenario, fixed. Don't try to change your man, obviously (use methods so subtle they remain blissfully and happily unaware of them). Men like to improve but not be improved, so love and encourage him and gently show him where he might be letting you down.

Life's a game of two hearts

Men and sport. They go together like strawberries and cream – make that beer and pretzels. It's a tribal thing. Men like to watch sport in packs, swear and swig. They shout unintelligible things at the screen, verbally execute the referee and canonise the scorer. They love it. You may not. But learning the rules, knowing the names of their superheroes and being able to discuss obscure offside rules and appreciate the sheer beauty of the game is a way to his heart. Give it a try. You may score, too.

Champagne and roses

Flowers and champagne work for both sexes. It's called Buck's Fizz after all and cacti are quite manly and spiky. Men like to feel desired. On Valentine's Day or his birthday, turn the tables and deliver a bottle of champagne in person to his office at the end of the day, dressed as provocatively as he would like or public transport and conventions will allow. Make him feel good in front of his envious colleagues. Go home and watch the bubbles rise. It worked for Marilyn Monroe. Happy Birthday, Mr Vice-President.

Turn him into a screen lover

Spend a Saturday night at home listening to your guy's favourite music or watching his choice of movie. It may well be an action/horror film in which more people lose their lives or limbs than their hearts, but tell him it is his night. Pretend to really enjoy it. If it is really dull, tell him half-way through that you forgot to mention that you are wearing that special lingerie he bought you and The End may be different and the credits will roll. Don't forget the popcorn.

Be his dream woman

Turn your man's fantasy into reality. Discover his dream woman and get her round (metaphorically speaking). Buy him a ticket to her concert or arrange for a signed photograph. Arrange a look-alike to come to a surprise party for him. Buy a karaoke machine, have some singing lessons and give a fabulous rendition of his favourite song in the style of his fantasy woman. Buy a costume and greet him by surprise. Stun, seduce and blow him away with your performance. Turn the lights out for extra authenticity.

Tell him why you love him so

Wake him up on a Sunday morning with breakfast in bed, all the newspapers and a little note saying 'Ten Things I Love About You.' Or fewer if ten prove too challenging. Tell him the day is his. He can do what he wants, go where he likes, eat whatever he fancies. Make him feel like a King Guy, even if he chooses to be a Super Slob, chain-watching sport, all the remotes lined up, pizza boxes and chilled beer at his side. Give him an Indian head massage and a pedicure as he relaxes.

Let him be your superhero

Men like to come to the rescue of women in distress. Beneath every man's suit is a Superhero outfit, stretched in some places as he gets older but still intact and ready for use. Make him feel like he is the only guy in town who can get the car started, who can mow the lawn, who can fix the plumbing. You are so strong, you are so talented, you are so efficient – learn all these phrases and use them to get what you want. He feels like the handsome guy in the cape, you get the jobs done. Sorted.

Is his Heart Really in it?

There are ways of spotting if your relationship is in trouble. Keep an eye and an ear out for them – you may be able to detect if your man's heart is really in it long before he'll admit it to you (or perhaps even before he admits it to himself). Then try to bring it out into the open: it might prompt a useful discussion of what is going wrong. It could also indicate that he is not the man for you. Peruse below and choose whether or not to lose your fellow. Talk the talk or walk the walk...

Food for Love

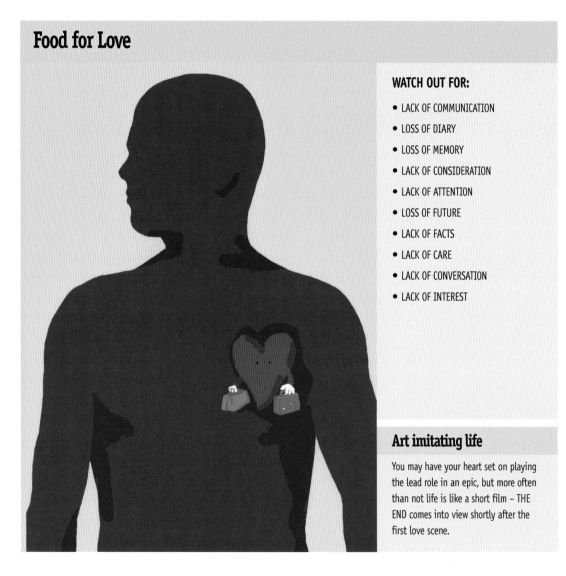

WATCH OUT FOR:

- LACK OF COMMUNICATION
- LOSS OF DIARY
- LOSS OF MEMORY
- LACK OF CONSIDERATION
- LACK OF ATTENTION
- LOSS OF FUTURE
- LACK OF FACTS
- LACK OF CARE
- LACK OF CONVERSATION
- LACK OF INTEREST

Art imitating life

You may have your heart set on playing the lead role in an epic, but more often than not life is like a short film – THE END comes into view shortly after the first love scene.

Silence isn't golden

If you don't hear from your man for days on end, something is up and it is not the phone bill. No texts, emails, letters or calls indicate that he has other issues on his mind or screen. He could have gone AWOL – absent without love.

When was your birthday again?

He doesn't buy you a birthday or Valentine's Day card. He forgets that you first met this day last year. You may well not be the first person on his mind, and if you are not careful you could end up first person singular.

Who were you again?

He is horrid to you or ignores you in front of his mates. He criticises you openly in public, riding roughshod over your feelings. He doesn't introduce you to his friends.
You need to have words or he could be out on his ear.

Get his number

He spends ages chatting to another girl at a party and takes her phone number. Blatantly, secretly – it doesn't really make a difference. She is in her little black dress and in his little black book. He deserves to be in your bad one.

U-turn if you want to

Guys heads turn 360 degrees sometimes when they see an attractive girl in the street. They claim it is to do with their lack of peripheral vision. If his eyes and tongue almost fall out of his head regularly, he may be setting his sights elsewhere.

Any future?

You suggest booking a relaxing break together for later in the year. The price is great, the venue and timing perfect, but he shows no enthusiasm for making a decision about it. Will you be together then? You may both be thinking the same thing.

Only the nose knows

You ask him where he was last night. He licks his lips nervously, his voice goes all squeaky and he keeps touching his nose. He could be lying. He could be nervous. You need to talk or buy a lie detector.

No concern of his

Something upsets you deeply and he is not interested or concerned. He sweeps your worries aside to make room for his own. You may well have trouble finding room for you in his me, me, me world.

We don't talk any more

You go out for a meal and the conversation dries up before the starter arrives. Nothing you say sparks a dialogue. He makes no effort to talk. Forget the dessert, this could become an emotional desert.

C U later

You can't think of a 'C' word that fits your relationship. Conversation, compromise, concern, commitment – none of them apply any more. Try to find out why but you may have to kiss it goodbye. 'Ciao baby' starts with 'C' too.

Ideal Man

Love at First Sight?

Don't close your door on Mr Right if he's late arriving. And don't rule certain guys out if bells don't start ringing and angels singing in the sky when you first meet.

Chance Encounters

You never know where you might meet Mr Right. At a party, gig, bookshop or in the waiting room at the dentist. It could happen any time, any place, just when you least expect it.

'The world is half full of men. Therefore, every woman has more than half a chance of finding her sole mate.'
BARBARA HOLMES, MATHEMATICIAN, 1960

Think Smart
One of the best ways of getting to know new guys is through friends of friends. But try not to judge people by first impressions. They could be having a bad hair/skin/dress day.

Charm Offensive
Look relaxed, confident, amusing, interested and positive when you meet new people. Try not to look desperate, dull or down in the mouth. You may get a negative response.

Looking for Mr Right

Birds do it, bees do it, even your parents (oh please!) must have done it. Humans, animals, birds, even fleas, look for love. The big question is: is there a soul mate out there waiting or actively looking? Is there really a Mr Right? Are there a number of Mr Rights, a few Mr Nearly Rights, a sprinkling of Mr Right Enoughs and a handful Mr All Right on the Nights? Women are likely to come across a few Mr Wrongs in their time – it comes with the territory. It's part of the pursuit of the perfect person.

Sometimes it's hard to imagine what Mr Right will look and be like, if and when he turns up. The next two chapters should help you on that score, with their gallery of possibilities. No need to scour the bars, clubs, stores, bookshops, workplace or salsa clubs for inspiration. Peruse the profiles that follow in this chapter, meander through the Manscellany (see page 100), glance at the gallery of guys – whether ideal or not, right for you or wrong for you. Check out the chaps. You might pick out The One in the line up. Alternatively, you could save valuable time by eliminating The Wrong One at the initial research stage.

Everyone knows they may have to snog a frog or two before puckering with their prince. Finding The One can take time but you might as well make the most of the experience. Remember that, unlike dogs and cats, humans are not perfect. We all have shortcomings of some sort, whether physical, emotional, intellectual, dental or conversational. Some men think they are without fault but therefore tend towards arrogance and self-obsession. Being perfect takes a serious amount of time and attention to the self. You may feel he goes where huge egos go – into the box marked Beware, Dangerous Levels of Toxic Substances. Let the egos sumo-wrestle together and leave that box well alone.

It might help to list the qualities you are looking for in your ideal man. You can then tick a few boxes when you meet someone – and see if you are still ticking them once you are deeper into the relationship and perhaps after you are committed partners. Don't go to a party or club and start giving potential candidates marks out of ten on the spot, list in one hand, pen in another. The chances of mating with your soul mate may plummet to zero. Eight out of ten ain't bad, so don't expect a full house when he does show up. Bingo.

When thinking of your Ideal Man, consider the attributes of someone you already admire and feel affection for. Ask yourself what it is that attracts you to your friends. Ask them what they think your perfect partner would be like. They see you from the outside. You know yourself from the inside. A different viewpoint could help. Try to think why a past relationship did not work out. What was it about Mr Not Right that you liked or did not like? What made you incompatible? What did you learn about yourself?

PERFECT PETER

Perfect Peter may take his time arriving. Don't expect him to know your address – show him the way.

Don't expect Superman to land on your doorstep or balcony, take you in his strong arms and whisk you away to a perfect sunset. Life is rarely like that sadly. Mr Right might not have a cape and a thigh-hugging suit encasing rippling muscles, but he could be The One. Remember, even Superman had an Achilles heel.

Describe Mr Right...

Romantic/Raunchy/Reliable/Rich
Interesting/Intellectual/Inspirational/Irrepressible
Generous/Gorgeous/Groovy/Gallant
Hunky/Humorous/Handsome/Hardworking
Thoughtful/Tantric/Tempting/Tantalising

Weak-kneed/Wilful/Waspish/Wobble-butted
Rampaging/Repressed/Restricting/Repulsive
Off-hand/Offensive/Opportunistic/Overpowering
Non-committal/Nasty/Needy/Nihilistic
Greedy/Gruesome/Grasping/Groping

WHICH OF THE FOLLOWING ATTRACT YOU IN A MAN?

A) BIG, SOULFUL EYES
B) WASHBOARD STOMACH
C) LARGE, BULGING WALLET
D) ENORMOUS INTELLECT
E) HUGE HEART
F) BIG FEET
G) STRONG NOSE
H) SENSUAL MOUTH
I) POWERFUL CAR

WHAT PUTS YOU OFF IN A MAN?

A) NARROW EYES
B) SNUB NOSE
C) FLABBY STOMACH
D) TINY FEET
E) SMALL HOUSE
F) TIGHT WALLET
G) NO CAR
H) NO HAIR
I) NO TEETH

HOW MANY MR WRONGS HAVE YOU MET?

A) ZERO
B) 1–5
C) 5–10
D) 10–15
E) OVER 15
F) LOST COUNT
G) NEED A CALCULATOR
H) CAN'T GET ENOUGH OF THEM

WHICH OF THE FOLLOWING IS YOUR TYPE OF SUPERHERO?

A) SUPERMAN
B) BATMAN
C) MR INCREDIBLE
D) ROBIN HOOD
E) ROBIN
F) TARZAN
G) SPIDERMAN
H) JAMES BOND
I) CHAMPION THE WONDERHORSE
J) NONE OF THE ABOVE

DO YOU BELIEVE IN LOVE AT FIRST SIGHT?

A) ABSOLUTELY
B) ABSOLUTELY NOT
C) I USED TO
D) STILL WAITING TO BE CONVINCED
E) YES, EVERY TIME IT HAPPENS
E) NEVER

Man Spotting

Spotting Mr Right requires a certain amount of knowledge of the species itself. Men come in all shapes, sizes and age groups. There is a standard model but a million versions with hidden pluses and minuses. Some engines are more powerful than others and some come with in-built music systems and remote controls, but they get to operate them.

Let's start the study with a spot of history. Have a look at the how men have developed over the ages and give each one marks out of ten.

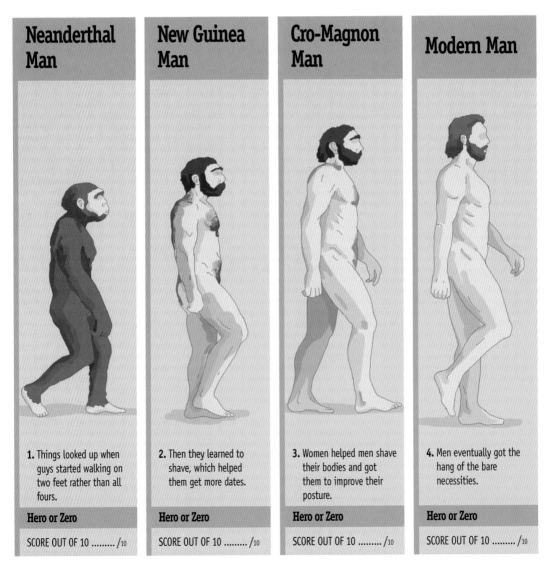

Neanderthal Man

1. Things looked up when guys started walking on two feet rather than all fours.

Hero or Zero

SCORE OUT OF 10 .... /10

New Guinea Man

2. Then they learned to shave, which helped them get more dates.

Hero or Zero

SCORE OUT OF 10 .... /10

Cro-Magnon Man

3. Women helped men shave their bodies and got them to improve their posture.

Hero or Zero

SCORE OUT OF 10 .... /10

Modern Man

4. Men eventually got the hang of the bare necessities.

Hero or Zero

SCORE OUT OF 10 .... /10

An Age-Old/Old-Age Question

The age group you go for is up to you of course. The old debate of Older Man vs. Toy Boy as opposed to Someone Your Own Age rumbles on. Experience vs. Stamina – it's up to you to find out the score on that one. Don't confuse Older Man with Prehistoric Man,

unless you fancy all the trimmings that go with a Mr Neanderthal. It's a different kind of hunting, shooting and fishing lifestyle on offer from him. Some of the men shown below are very old indeed. You might want to think twice about dating them.

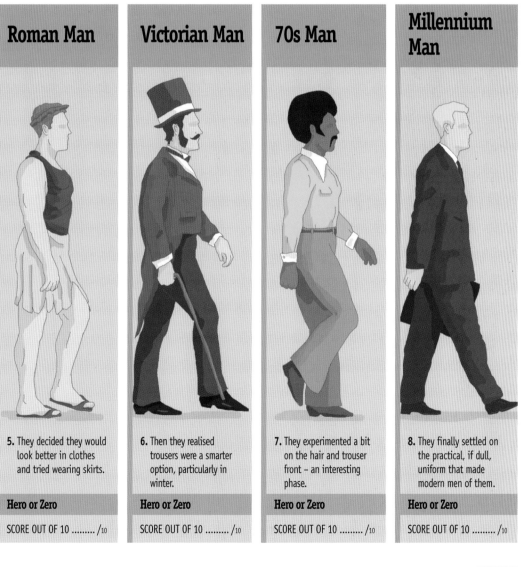

Roman Man	Victorian Man	70s Man	Millennium Man
5. They decided they would look better in clothes and tried wearing skirts.	**6.** Then they realised trousers were a smarter option, particularly in winter.	**7.** They experimented a bit on the hair and trouser front – an interesting phase.	**8.** They finally settled on the practical, if dull, uniform that made modern men of them.
Hero or Zero	**Hero or Zero**	**Hero or Zero**	**Hero or Zero**
SCORE OUT OF 10 .... /10	SCORE OUT OF 10 .... /10	SCORE OUT OF 10 .... /10	SCORE OUT OF 10 .... /10

DIY Mr Right

OK, so now you have taken the first steps on the road to finding Mr Right by completing the questionnaire and studying a little of the history of the male mystery on the previous pages, it's time to take things to the next level. Let's really visualise. Visualisation can trigger realisation. Picturing your ideal kind of guy in your mind's eye makes him potentially viable rather than just vaguely possible. He's a concrete thought, not just a dreamy idea. You will start to realise him and to make him a reality. If he's doing the same thing and you are both in the right place at the right time, then bingo… that's how love happens.

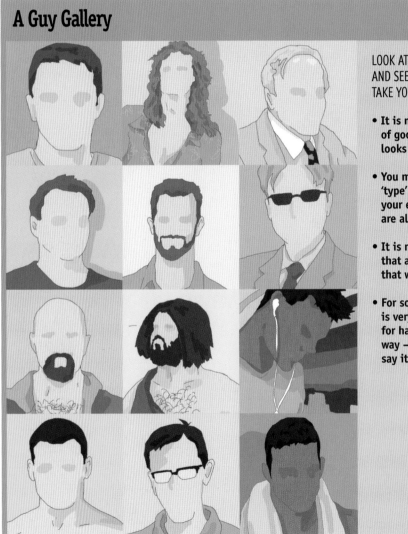

A Guy Gallery

LOOK AT THIS GALLERY OF GUYS AND SEE WHICH ONE (OR ONES) TAKE YOUR FANCY:

- It is not always a question of good looks but the right looks for you.

- You may well not have a 'type' at all – think back to your exes and see if they are all similar or dissimilar.

- It is more about the look that appeals than the look that wins the prizes.

- For some the *joli-laid* look is very attractive (French for handsome in an ugly way – careful how you say it).

Mix and match

Different women have different priorities when defining their Mr Right. Some women like bulging muscles and wallets. Others put bulging brains ahead of large bank accounts. It all depends where you like your bulges, really. Some guys make you laugh and think deeply, and also pay the bill. Others pay the bill but don't make you smile much. Others share the same jokes and the bills. The world is full of different women and men. Imagine your own Greek god and what order his attributes would come in.

What Does Your Greek God Have?

PUT IN ORDER OF IMPORTANCE (1–6) THE FOLLOWING:

- ☐ BRAINS
- ☐ BRAWN
- ☐ GOOD SENSE OF HUMOUR
- ☐ GREAT PERSONALITY
- ☐ EMOTIONAL AWARENESS AND SENSITIVITY
- ☐ DRESS SENSE

DIY man kit

But first, think how wonderful it would be if you could walk into a hardware store and buy a DIY Man Kit. You could build your own Greek god, selecting the body parts you find most appealing in terms of size, strength, youthfulness and healthiness, the brain you find most fascinating and seductive, and the biggest heart you could ever wish to pick. How fab would it be if you could take individual parts back and swop them for different ones, having tried them on and found them wanting? Imagine how satisfying it would be to say things like, 'His legs are too short, sorry, and I didn't like the way he moved when I got him home. I'd like one with bigger pecs and a better sense of humour, and hold the hairy toes.'

Would you like your man gift-wrapped?

Imagine the scenario when you get to the counter in the first place: 'Can I help you, Madam?' – 'Yes, please. I would like Brad Pitt's body, Einstein's brain, Richard Branson's bank balance, Bob Marley's musical genius and Shakespeare's way with words.' 'OK, Madam, you can pick up your kit at the check-out in about ten minutes. Will you be paying cash and would you like him gift-wrapped?' Take some time to think what your DIY Man Kit would contain. Just think of the fun you will have assembling him and then taking him apart again.

Write a list of those features, both physical and emotional, that you find most important. Men place more emphasis on looks and first impressions than women do, generally speaking, but there's no harm in thinking what your ideal man would look like if you could get to choose each body part. If you have a partner, look at a photograph and imagine what he would look like with bigger thighs, longer hair, a slimmer stomach, smaller butt. What would you change if the DIY Manstore was still open? Don't ever let him know...

Visualise to realise

If you can't envisage Mr Right, it will be very hard for you to identify him when he walks into the room. He will have had to park his white horse outside, so that won't be a sign. Wearing a full set of shining armour, complete with glistening sword and shield, is only going to work at a fancy dress party. A T-shirt saying 'I'm The One for You' will simply put you off by being a mixture of cheesy and obvious. Try doing a sketch – whether in your mind or on paper. Thumb through the gallery on the next few pages and see if you spot something you like. Write down the page numbers with the most appealing guys on. Show them to your girlfriends or your best male friend (see page 104) to see what they think of your choice. A few no-no's have been included as deterrents, decoys or diversions, just to keep you on your toes. Don't worry, you'll soon get the picture.

Mr Just Not Real

Is there such a thing as a perfect match? Are women searching for Mr Perfect, looking for Mr Right (For Them) or settling for Mr Nearly Right? Imagine you have just walked into Men 'R' Us. Would you head for the aisle marked Perfect Goods or make for Good Deals of the Day instead? Wouldn't it be fabulous if you could buy one, get one free? Being serious, though, someone with no faults, foibles, fallibilities or fatty areas may only serve to make you more aware of yours, unless you are lucky enough to have none of the above, in which case it is a perfect match in all senses. Browse through the following as if you were looking at a catalogue. Imagine you are doing so on the internet. Select your own e-male, put him in your basket and go to check-out. Get the low down and then download. The rest is up to you.

Head and shoulders (above the vest)

Not a (nose) hair out of place, not a zit or a razor cut on his face, let's put Mr Perfectly Formed or Mr Just Not Real in his place. He will probably have a good head of hair, dark eyes, a strong nose and an angular jaw. His features, like his body, are more than likely to be totally symmetrical (symmetry of face and body plays a role in our attraction and attractiveness, as an indicator of health, fitness and beauty, apparently). If you were to draw a horizontal line down the middle of his face (no, not with your eyeliner), both sides would be mirror images. Try it on a photo of yourself, your partner or your dream media star or footballer. The width of Mr Perfect'ss face should be five times that of his eyes, with one eye space between them – the eyes that is. This may come as a surprise to some guys who consider themselves naturally perfect creations. But before you fall for Mr Perfect, go back to your school days and remember Narcissus from Greek mythology; he spent so much time gazing longingly at his own reflection in a pool that he wasted away with unrequited love for himself. Make sure Mr Perfect has enough love left over for you. Make sure the so-called exclusive relationship involves both of you and not just Mr P and his mirror image. Check out the brain power and conversational skills too – he may be more Men's Mags than Mensa. And is he perfectly funny? Does he make you laugh (intentionally)?

Torso talking

Mr Perfect's physique will be well-shaped (see page 10), and he will sport big, strong shoulders, a broad chest, slim hips and excellent muscle tone. He won't bulge with biceps as big as lead balloons, but he will be toned, taut and tanned, sculpted, shaped and streamline. He will be dressed to impress and progress. He will be impeccable. Talking of pecs, his may be hairless, along with his shoulders and back (ouch) and even his calves. He will pack an impressive 6-pack. He will gleam with freshly moisturised skin and smell as fresh and fragrant as you do after bathing luxuriously with expensive oils.

He will be no stranger to day spas and may spend more on cosmetics than you. None of this is too critical of and in itself, as they say, but if Mr Perfect spends too much time on his own body, will he have any time, interest or stamina left for yours? Does his torso contain enough heart for both of you? If he starts giving you skin care advice and suggesting a back wax, you need to talk. If he suggests you are losing your arm candy appeal, you may need to walk. Hide your expensive anti-wrinkle cream or he will use dollops on his butt. Talking of which…

Below the belt

Mr Perfect's rear assets will be small, firm and steely. Many women will want to pinch his butt, in both senses, so watch out. Holding onto Mr Perfect can be taxing in lots of ways, and you will have to be fit enough to keep up, again in both senses. You may have to decide if it is worth the effort. If you view your relationship as a personal investment, you will need to monitor just what sort of returns you are getting. This is where the G-factor comes in. There are two sorts of generosity: financial and emotional. Is he generous both of wallet and spirit? The latter is harder to define than the former and for many, more important. Mr Perfect is only truly worthy of the name if he allows you access to his emotional resources as well as his financial ones when necessary. Does he get his heart out as much as his wallet or are both covered in cobwebs? Does he wear his feelings on his sleeve as much as he sports labels on his designer jeans? That's the bottom line for some. Does he buy you two dozen immaculate roses when a hug and a kiss were all you really wanted. Some of you will want him to be loaded in the front assets zone. That's a matter of taste. By the way, Mr Perfect's shoes will be polished (so he can see his reflection) and expensive, like him. Would marriage be a meeting of minds and bodies? Would he have time for Master or Mistress Perfect?

The Overview

The Look

Preened and polished –
everything about this guy
screams 'Look at me!' (which
is exactly what he spends his
own time doing).

Top Marks

Tanned and chiselled, he has
a V-shaped torso. V for Vain.
Going to the gym is his priority
number one.

Body Talk

Always on display and shown
to best effect, his body is a
challenge to others. It says
'Beat this for perfection.'

Legging It

Smart, dark jeans, always worn
with a chunky belt. But do they
hide spindly legs that fail to
match the gym-perfect torso?

Sole to Soul

Black leather and always
polished to a perfect finish.
He likes what he sees in the
mirror shine – sadly, you
may not.

N.B.

Not a candidate for a long-term
relationship, this is an I.L.M.
or O.F.F. guy (I Love Me/OK For
a Fling).

Mr Good Deal

Shopping expeditions, like parties or nights out, are always more fun when you come home with a really good deal. Some of you will already have bagged yours, others may still be checking out those on offer or waiting for new stock to come in. As we determined earlier, men shop differently from women, infusing the process with less emotion and often treating it as an exercise. Similarly, some men see bagging their women in a different way. Many appear to place more emphasis, at least in the initial phases, on physical rather than emotional or intellectual attributes. Ever heard a guy on the street shout, 'Oi, look at the enormous brain on her?' For many women, a sensitive, supportive, caring and understanding male is just as attractive one with a good face and body. Quality control in purchases from the Men 'R' Us store is getting stricter and more demanding...

Head and shoulders (above the vest)

Mr Good Deal is not a high maintenance, top-drawer, luxury item, gift-wrapped in impeccable style. His physique and features will probably be a little less symmetrical than those of his predecessor, Mr Just Not Real. His smile may be crooked, his eyes more (or less) than five eyes apart, his ears could be large (he's a good listener) or small (he won't hear a word said against you) and his stubble is unintentional, his goatee or beard endearing. His hair may be messy, doing a disappearing act or already history, and his moisturising and beauty regime somewhat hit and miss. Mr GD's eyebrows won't be mirror images, groomed to perfection, but his eyes will be sympathetic, kind and sensitive and make you feel safe and secure. They won't have a roaming contract or compulsion, they will be there just for you. He will admire you more often than his own reflection. His nose may be too small or large for his face, it may even have been broken in a pitch battle. It will still fit on his face quite comfortably, as will his mouth, which will be kind and kissable, if not perfectly formed. When you look at Mr GD 's features, you may think 'hey, come here cute guy', but when you examine your motives and his features, it could be as a result of the positive emotions triggered than the physical attributes displayed. And he has a great sense of humour and knows how to talk to you. Result.

Torso talking

Mr Good Deal may not have a perfect V for a torso, with impressively strong, manly shoulders tapering to neatly narrow hips. He may or may not – maybe he did one day; it is not the most important thing about his physique, for you at least, because he has the X factor. A powerful upper torso gives the impression that a man is a protector, ready at any moment to lift a damsel over his shoulder, plucking her from imminent danger and distress. That used to work for women when sabre-toothed tigers lurked outside the home, but it is less vital to survival nowadays. If a man is all muscle and no feeling, then what use is a caveman's lift anyway? If a car has a turbo-charged engine but no emotional fuel running through its system, then where

can it transport you? You'll be a passenger going nowhere, unmoved by the man in the driving seat. Mr GD's biceps may not bulge but his heart will. He will be sensitive to your feelings and moods, he will care if you are unhappy, he will be supportive, giving, considerate and thoughtful. He will think for two, not just for himself. Commitment is not a terrifying word for him. He will dress casually and there may be toothpaste on his jacket, but who cares? And he will love dogs and children, which makes him husband and father material.

Below the belt

What goes on below the waist is not the most important thing about Mr GD. His rear assets may need a little fine tuning but lots of loving can help on that score. Rippling, Schwarzenegger-like muscles may not lurk under slightly worn or torn jeans, but you will feel comfortable with his body, rather than intimidated by it or exhausted by the need to be as fit and faultless as him. All males are made of puppy dog tails as we know, and their size will vary from Pekingese to German Shepherd via French Poodle. This is perhaps less important than the percentage of slug involved, and Mr Good Deal is comparatively low on slug and snail content. The size of his assets (financial, emotional or puppy dog tail) won't matter much to you. He is a good deal in all those areas. His wallet will be regularly used, cobwebs nowhere in sight, and, more valuably, he will spend time and effort on you. Generous of spirit and pocket, that's a good deal. He may not flex muscle and pump iron at the gym to form carved calves, but he will expend energy and gain points by enjoying walks and other joint activities with you. His shoes may not be leather mirrors (see Mr Perfect's footwear) but nor will he sport dull grey slip-ons. Sneakers or loafers are more his style – unpolished, not showy or designer-led, but comfortable and stylish – that's him. He will nod at fashion trends but shake his head at being a fashion victim.

The Overview

The Look

He looks relaxed and confident, but not overly so. His general temperament is approachable and sensitive.

Body Talk

His body language is open and welcoming, rather than closed off or hostile. It says 'Hi, nice to see you.'

Sole to Soul

His footwear is comfortable and practical, but not stuffy. It says 'I'm quietly stylish but not a slave to style.'

Top Marks

He has a medium build, with broad shoulders, and a willingness to embrace your worries as well as his own.

Legging It

For that smart-casual look, he'll tend to stick to jeans that are clean, practical and attractive (much like his genes).

N.B.

Overall, he's a winner – not perfect, but way above average. This is a N.P.M. or G.F.I. guy (Nearly Perfect Match /Go For It).

Mr Raw Deal

When Men 'R' Us announces its annual sale, the rush for Mr Perfect and Mr Good Deal will leave Mr Raw Deal lurking on the shelves until the last day, when stock is offered at a knock-down, everything-must-go (somewhere) price. An unsuspecting purchaser will go home with what they imagine is a real bargain and find out too late that this is a no returns guy in every sense. She should have tried him on for size at the store. Mr Raw Deal is just that. In some ways, he is much more than many women will have bargained for and in others much less of a man than she thought he would be. Watch out because some men develop into a raw deal after starting life as an attractive one. Keep tabs on him or you might wake up one day in possession of one, without ever having put him on your shopping list.

Head and shoulders (above the vest)

Mr Raw Deal's face is an indicator of his life's style and mantra. It speaks volumes through its lack of care and attention, its unintentional, unappealing four-day stubble, neglected skin, hangdog eyes, dirty hair and saggy cheeks. It says 'I am a slob. No job or emotional concern is too small for me to turn down or too big for me to ignore.' Any redeeming features will be lost behind the unkempt façade. Nose hair may sprout, eyebrows join, zits and boils compete for squatting rights. He has become a stranger to you and to shampoo, to clean and cream, to caring and sharing. You are in the presence of Mr Raw Deal. He is positively negative. If you are within spitting distance of him domestically, you may wonder how it came to this. He does not spend all day looking in the mirror, but he does think of himself first, you second or maybe third or fourth, after television, beer and sport. He doesn't talk much, he doesn't ask how you are, he doesn't help in the house, he doesn't make you laugh, except when he suggests that he is still a hunky beast chased by other women. What? Around the sofa, where he spends most of his day? Dream on Mr RD...

Torso talking

The torso is the bit below the neck and above the belt, by the way. You may need a chart to help you locate it in the case of Mr Raw Deal, whose contours will be difficult to identify and not because you're bad at reading maps. See Mr Perfect and Mr Good Deal for map references. Mr RD is not sculpted, chiselled or V-shaped. His shoulders and stomach meet somewhere in the middle to form an embarrassed O-shape, he resembles the lump of clay before the sculptor started work (don't try to make it better with a hammer) but he exercises – his remote hand and his beer arm. A six-pack is what he uses to fill his paunch not structure it, pumping iron means eating more steak and keeping fragrant, fresh and smooth is 'for girls'. Dumbbells are the girls he watches on his DVDs and lunges are only performed in extreme circumstances when the referee on the screen needs a good kicking. His conversational skills are limited to non-sofa slob moments, and his heart so preoccupied with surviving a regime of poor diet and lack of exercise that it has little time to open up to others. He is emotionally constipated. Is this description going unfortunately below the belt? We are now...

Below the belt

Mr Raw Deal is unlikely to make up for his failings in the other departments by being outstanding in this zone. A lack of generosity of spirit and little instinct to care and share and be sensitive to the needs of others may not be redeemed by being loaded in his back or front pocket. His rear assets may slump through lack of activity, and he won't score on the fashion front, unless you like vests, baggy shirts and sagging, tracksuit bottoms or jeans that groan when done up. He dresses for horizontal or semi-slumped comfort and ease of manoeuvre from bar stool to sofa, not to impress or promote himself vertically, either domestically or professionally. He lacks motivation together with outdoor hobbies or interests; his indoor interests rarely involve vacuuming the stairs or bounding gazelle-like up them to embrace other activities in the love department. Mr Raw Deal is negatively negative downstairs and rarely positively positive upstairs. He wears no shoes for most of the day or dirty trainers as out of fashion as the rest of his wardrobe. Is he really husband material?

The Overview

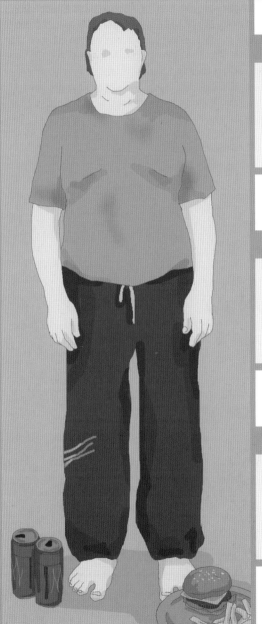

The Look

This guy is a slob. Everything about him says 'Please wash me.' Don't offer to – you wouldn't enjoy it.

Body Talk

Lethargic, lumbering and lacking poise. His body language says 'I have given up making any effort.'

Sole to Soul

No footwear worn indoors, and maybe the odd smelly old sock hanging around his sofa – it says it all.

Top Marks

Lacking in muscle and carrying more than a few extra pounds. He can only just support his own head and body weight; he won't be there for you.

Legging It

Old, stained jogging bottoms – never actually used for jogging. At least they're better than seeing what lurks beneath...

N.B.

Not that you would ever want to, but this guy is definitely a H.U.G. (Hygienically Undesirable Guy).

Mr No Deal

Think back to prehistoric times when Cavemen 'R' Us took over the site of Dinosaurs 'R' Us. What sort of guy would have been on offer? Upright but only just, he was probably still more vertical than Mr Raw Deal. The men in the aisles would have been protector-providers in the old style, and women shoppers would have selected their mates by size of muscle, location of cave, likelihood of healthy offspring and hunter-gathering/DIY skills. Mr Caveman's way with tools was vital for survival. Today, however, consumer choice is less limited, although there are still a few Fred Flintstones around, complete with dinosaur pet. Barney Pre-man or Brad Pitt – hmmm, you may need a moment to decide. Instead of guy-next-door, Mr No Deal is rather guy-past-age. The protector-provider has a certain appeal for women, but loincloths went out long ago (although fur jockstraps may still be in fashion in some caves). Most women have rejected prehistoric behaviour, and some men need to wake up and smell the coffee in the marble and steel minimalist kitchen, not the rotting meat bones in the fur-carpeted cave.

Head and shoulders (above the vest)

Mr No Deal could also be called Mr No Truck with Modern Trends. He will wash and shave when he needs to, but he will pluck and moisturise as often as he visits a spa or spots a sabre-tooth tiger in the garden. He goes for the He-Man look; the 'Me Man, You Woman' approach is his primary instinct. His features are probably angular and striking, his face not necessarily five eyes wide and there will be little symmetry to his face or his thinking. Rather than a left vs. right set of features, it will be an 'I'm always right' mindset. Mr No Deal is very much in touch with his masculine side. He has little truck with his feminine side and finds it hard to get really into yours, emotionally speaking. He may well sport stubble, he will be manly, his brain will be in masculine gear and he probably thinks a metrosexual is a form of public transport for swingers. He needs help coming to terms with the 21st century but his heart is in the right place, even if his brain is not in the same gear as yours.

Torso talking

The message is clear from Zone Torso. Muscles will be to the fore, hairy chest on display, broad shoulders bristling, upper arms a force to be reckoned with, hands large and undeniably manly. Men generally like to be in control and Mr No Deal takes this tendency extremely seriously. His advances won't be very advanced (it's an age-old complaint), his seduction technique predates 'Me Tarzan, You Jane', but he will have a big heart under all that powerful muscle. If you like your men to be all man, then here he is. He is all testosterone so he may have less hair on his head than his torso, back and front. He is very much an alpha male, *Homo Erectus*-style. He believes in survival of the fittest and stays fit for that reason, but pumps Iron Age-style and raises dumbbells over his shoulder. He probably has a healthy heart – it just requires some evolution. Then it will be able to provide for you financially, physically and emotionally. He has an X chromosome (as do all males – they get it from their mothers) but he doesn't talk about it much. He loves his mother and he will provide a good home for you and the baby Flintstones, but you will have to choose the colour scheme.

Below the belt

Mr ND is a traditional hunter-gatherer, so his wallet will be willing, but he will leave the cooking to you. You will probably have to buy him some decent, up-to-the-era clothes. Left to his own devices, he would buy six sets of the same builders' bottom jeans or flammable track pants and match them with the same white T-shirt. Why not invest in some thigh-hugging, low-slung jeans to show off his front and rear assets – reap the rewards of his excellent genes and enjoy his impressive portfolio. He will wear functional clothes because he is an outdoors kind of guy. He excels at fixing, digging, constructing, demolishing, protecting and providing. He is very much a hands-on (sometimes feet first) man, both in the garden and the bedroom. You may need to train him in the love zone and teach him how to get in touch with your feminine needs. Mr No Deal (with flatpacks) will design and build himself a shed and then spend lots of time in it. If you need anything fixing in the home, you won't need to call in a professional. He loves you – he just needs to learn a few more handy tips. And he loves his pet dinosaur.

The Overview

The Look

Not the snappiest of dressers nor most enthusiastic of shoppers, he has the look of a historian – history is where he belongs.

Body Talk

His body language is overconfident, bordering on the hostile. His body doesn't verbalise much; it just shrugs.

Sole to Soul

Anything large and masculine, probably with steel toecaps. Feet first, feelings later – that's the motto.

Top Marks

He is pure muscle – top to toe. Not the most yielding of bodies, but great if you like brawn cocktails.

Legging It

His clothes, like him, are functional not fashionable. He wears the Manpower brand. Change the label if you have the willpower.

N.B.

Even if he's a big softy really, he's a N.G.B. (Nice Guy But...) with a B.N.B. (Brawn Not Brain) sub-clause.

Mr Men 'R' Us

There is an international smorgasbord of men out there – a selection of tasty dishes, new experiences, strange concoctions, unusual combinations and unidentifiable substances. Continuing the culinary theme, men are like roast chicken. Some parts are more appealing and succulent than others. Some women like nice firm golden thighs, others find a pumped-up, juicy chest area mouth-watering, and a few like to get their teeth into the parson's nose. If you could mix and match the best and worst bits of the various men in your life, just think what sort of a piece de resistance dish or disaster you could make. Come up with some concoctions of your own but glance at these first...

Good and Raw – No Deal

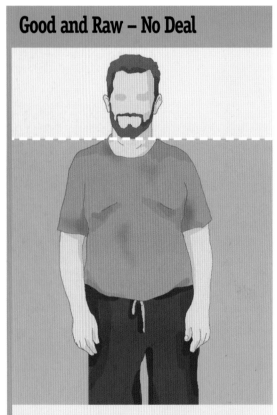

Good and raw works for food but not men. Take Mr Good Deal's thinking and feeling HQ and put it on Mr Raw Deal's physique and you have quite an interesting combination. Nurtured sensitivity plus mussel-muscle is not the perfect look. Sensitive slob? Hmm – think about it

No and Good – It's a Deal?

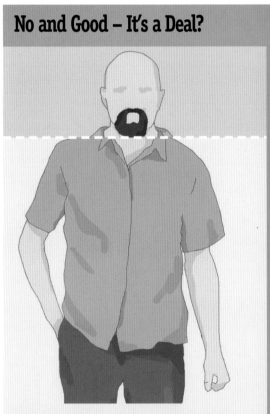

If you could put Mr Good Deal's head on Mr No Deal's body at least you would have some senstivity plus some muscle, a well defined sense of self and others plus a nice pair of pecs even in a slobby T-shirt. But Mr No Deal's emotions and Mr Good Deal's body is a bit of a halfway house (or relaxed bungalow).

The Fit Theory

Is your man a true fit? Does his top half match his lower half, or is he a bit of a misfit? Is he Mr Fit or Misfit? Think of three guys you admire, adore or hero-worship, and take their various thirds (head and shoulders, shoulder to hip and hip to toe) and put them together. Juggle them around and see what you come up with. Then do the same with guys you dislike, detest or zero-worship. Mix and Match and enjoy the results – you might just be able to improve on the original.

Raw and Just Not Real – OK?

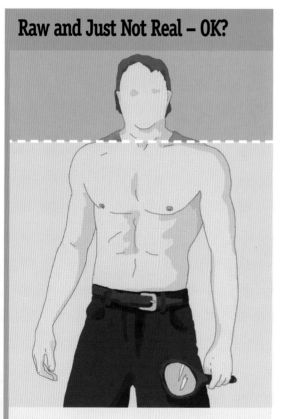

Now this is interesting. Put a H.U.G with an O.F.F. and you have got a good idea of what might happen. You would have lots of eye candy, but it would be horiontal on the couch all day. It seems quite a waste. What do you think?

Mr It's Up to You

This is the interactive part where you have to come up with your perfect combination and imagine what apsects of the Mr Deals you would select and assemble in one package. If you make a mistake, start from scratch. That is the best bit. Construct-Your-Man without the consequences. The perfect game...

♂ Manscellany

Spoilt for Choice
In this chapter, a variety of men submit their resumés for your perusal, approval or removal. There is lots of choice and quality control has got tighter.

Homo Sapiens
Just as in the animal kingdom, there are many species (and sub-species) of man. Find out about their natural habitats, diet, mating habits and plumage.

Take Your Time
Enjoy a gentle stroll through the guy gallery. There's no pressure or time schedule – think of it as speed-dating without the two-minute time limit.

'There are just over six billion people in the world. You have got a one in three billion chance of finding your one-in-a-million guy.'
LIZZIE STRACHAN-PARR, LECTURER IN STATISTICS, 2005

Call of the Wild
The Man-Spotter's Guide contains essential information on different types of men and will help you to recognise and assess a range of mating calls.

Introduction

The likelihood is that you will come across a whole array of different guy types as you make your way in that world, unless you decide to become a hermit and avoid them all. You will soon become aware that some men are more different than others, and that while a certain number are worthy of pursuit, love and commitment, an equal number are better avoided altogether. If only you could check out a chap remotely, without having to get your hands dirty. Well, your wish has been granted at last.

Think of the men you are about to meet on the following pages as candidates for your affection. Their applications come complete with pros and cons, so at the end of the virtual interview you can weigh up if they are the sort of guys you should be considering for a short- or long-term involvement. They might be bed and breakfast material or, instead, more suitable for greater investment with a view to future returns. Go through the portfolio of guys, or the Manscellany as it is called here, as if you were an investor looking to put your treasure in the right stock. See what is on the market, look at the good points and the bad points. As with all investments, it's the bottom line that matters. Yes or No? Only you can decide to go for it or move on to the next guy.

Before you make a decision, try the guys on for size. It's a try before you buy exercise. If only men were more like bras, then women could browse through the models on offer at their leisure, after being guided by experienced professionals about what is the right fit, try various designs on for size, find the perfect match and enjoy comfortable union, heart-to-heart support and intimate contact ever after. And one bra is never enough. Women need at least a couple to see them though the week. What could be better. Don't let men know they are being compared to bras. They like to take them off, not be taken off by them.

Having looked at the ideal man in principle in the previous chapter, it's time to get more specific about what Mr Right's day job will be. Tinker, tailor, soldier, sailor – we have all tried to determine the profession of our potential prince with prune stones. None of these professions appears in the Manscellany, but there are twelve guy types to peruse, choose or lose. That should keep you busy for a while. Find a quiet moment in your day, make yourself a nice hot beverage or pour yourself a glass of wine and go for it.

View this as a book you would normally find in the Natural History section of a book shop. Look for it next to a bird-spotter's guide. Like birdwatchers, you can tick off which species you have seen through your virtual binoculars. No need to lurk in wooden hides in the forest but you may have to be up and about early to spot some of the varieties. Keep an ear out for the mating call. If a particular type doesn't turn you on, turn a deaf ear and or a blind eye to him.

First, use the scorecard opposite to identify some of the facial features you like most. Mark each one out of ten so that you can make a quick judgement the next time a new model comes into view.

The 'Bra' Test

Men are like bras – both can make your life a nightmare if you choose the wrong one. Most women think carefully about whether or not to buy a particular bra, and are willing to make some ruthless (or at least objective) decisions about whether or not it comes up to scratch. So, when choosing a man, think about lingerie and ask yourself the following questions:

- **Does he look good?**
- **Will he make me look good?**
- **Is he a good fit?**
- **Does he make me feel comfortable?**
- **Is our relationship uplifting?**
- **Is he giving me enough support?**
- **Is he flexible?**
- **Will he give me a lift up in life or should we separate?**
- **Will he go saggy after a while?**
- **Will he need replacing soon?**

The Scorecard...

Cropped
SCORE OUT OF 10 .... /10

Sensible
SCORE OUT OF 10 .... /10

Bed-head
SCORE OUT OF 10 .... /10

Balding
SCORE OUT OF 10 .... /10

Clear Blue
SCORE OUT OF 10 .... /10

Dark Brown
SCORE OUT OF 10 .... /10

Perfect Green
SCORE OUT OF 10 .... /10

Cool Specs
SCORE OUT OF 10 .... /10

Fully Monty
SCORE OUT OF 10 .... /10

Top-Lip Only
SCORE OUT OF 10 .... /10

Sibeburns
SCORE OUT OF 10 .... /10

Goatee
SCORE OUT OF 10 .... /10

The Best Friend

The Best Friend is hard to find, but once identified he is an excellent species with which to spend time. Watch his behaviour in different environments and make notes. His plumage is casual and comfortable, his habits largely interesting and his behaviour friendly without being over-familiar, attractive without being threatening. Sometimes the Best Friend develops a strong affection for its spotter.

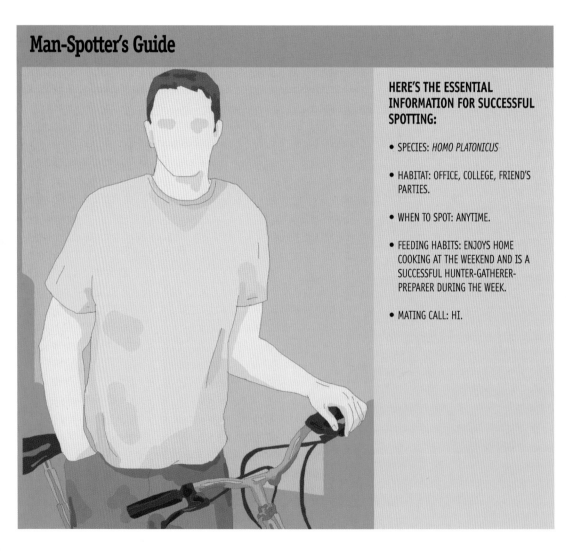

Man-Spotter's Guide

HERE'S THE ESSENTIAL INFORMATION FOR SUCCESSFUL SPOTTING:

- SPECIES: *HOMO PLATONICUS*

- HABITAT: OFFICE, COLLEGE, FRIEND'S PARTIES.

- WHEN TO SPOT: ANYTIME.

- FEEDING HABITS: ENJOYS HOME COOKING AT THE WEEKEND AND IS A SUCCESSFUL HUNTER-GATHERER-PREPARER DURING THE WEEK.

- MATING CALL: HI.

THE BEST FRIEND

NAME:	Johnny (aka JJ, John Boy, Johnny-pooh, Johnny darling)
DATE OF BIRTH:	Same year, same star sign (it's really weird)
OCCUPATION:	platonic friend and guy-next-door
ADDRESS:	Next door (duh!)

PERSONAL ATTRIBUTES:
Cute, friendly, popular, an excellent team player, reliable, punctual, always there when you need him, good in a crisis, easy to talk to, Johnny has a sympathetic ear, broad shoulders, a big heart, nice kind eyes and he's a great listener and social lubricant. Everybody likes Johnny. He's the kind of guy you could take home to meet your parents. He is polite, clever, hard-working, practical, clean, with no bad habits (and you are best friends and luckily he doesn't find you attractive so there's no problem on that front).

LOVE EXPERIENCE:
Johnny hasn't had any long term relationships because he hasn't met Miss Right yet. He has had a few romantic involvements but nothing serious. None of his girlfriends really appreciated him and always left him for someone more dangerous. Women really like spending time with Johnny but as soon as an exciting smooth operator comes along, they say they just want to be friends and head off into the sunset with the guy in the fast car with the designer sunglasses and the big apartment, who then dumps them. He's quite happy being single at the moment (which is great because I get to spend lots of time with him – in fact I think he really appreciates having a female friend like me).

FAVOURITE FILMS:
French films, anything with subtitles, comedy romances.

FAVOURITE MUSIC:
Pretty much likes anything from The Beatles to Bob Dylan.

FASHION STYLE:
Johnny wears casual, trendy clothes but is not a fashion victim. He gets some of his gear from thrift stores but looks cool in jeans and T-shirts with sneakers and attractive in his smart but relaxed suit for the publishing firm he works at.

DANCE STYLE:
Hip-hop meets funk but learning salsa.

INTERESTS AND HOBBIES:
Johnny loves books, movies, theatre, soccer, gigs, bars and clubs, weekends away, keeping fit, cycling to work (he doesn't believe in cars) and playing the guitar. He is a bit of an all-rounder and good at most things. He is also doing some creative writing. He doesn't like flashy stuff and is a bit of an environmentalist.

PETS:
Likes to go the pub with his parents' Labrador, when he goes home on Sundays.

BEST CHAT UP LINE:
'I don't suppose you fancy going to see a movie sometime, do you?' or 'I really like and respect you'.

FANTASY LOVE LOCATION:
Remote, romantic beach at sunset, soft wind blowing.

ANY DISTINGUISHING MARKS:
Big, blue eyes.

MOST ENDEARING HABIT:
Everything he does is endearing.

WORST HABIT:
None.

REMINDS YOU OF:
Ewan McGregor.

PROS AND CONS
Platonic friendships with guys are comforting, reassuring and rewarding, and are often much easier than romantic ones, once any whiff of sexual tension has evaporated or been extinguished. Platonic friends rely on each other for friendship, companionship and comfort and can be a great relationship of equals. However, once one person develops a romantic relationship with a third person, jealousy can arise. The new girlfriend could be jealous of a guy's female friends, you can become jealous of the new girlfriend, and the guy is often stuck in the middle and forced to choose who he spends time with.

LOVE POTENTIAL:
Yes and no.

The Guy at Work

This male is very common and is identifiable by his undistinguished and uninteresting appearance. His plumage is largely grey, to match his behaviour patterns. He is the master of camouflage and can sometimes make himself disappear completely from the naked eye. He has few distinguishing features except for the occasional choice of a showy tie or pair of socks (especially at Christmas parties).

Man-Spotter's Guide

HERE'S THE ESSENTIAL INFORMATION FOR SUCCESSFUL SPOTTING:

- SPECIES: *HOMO OFFICUS BORINGUS*

- HABITAT: OFFICE, COFFEE SHOP, PUB, GOLF-CLUB BAR.

- WHEN TO SPOT: 8.59 AM – 5.29 PM.

- FEEDING HABITS: HIS DIET IS POOR, LARGELY COMPOSED OF PRE-PACKAGED MEALS AND TAKE-OUTS. UNLIKELY TO TRY TO COOK HIS OWN FOOD AND NOT THAT KEEN ON FRUIT AND VEGETABLES.

- MATING CALL: HELLOOOO.

THE GUY AT WORK

NAME:	Steve (calls himself The Stud but nobody else does)
DATE OF BIRTH:	Wore flares first time round (and they are still going strong)
OCCUPATION:	Sales Exec
ADDRESS:	Nice two-bedroom house in the suburbs with a small garden

PERSONAL ATTRIBUTES:
Steve is divorced with a daughter (never tells you how old she is though). He likes to act the experienced man about town and 'hang' with the younger girls at work, but he is only just managing to hang onto his own hair and job. Over-friendly, over-familiar and almost over-the-love-hill, that's Steve all over. He has worked in the sales department for years, mostly on the road to start with, but now, sadly for all, he is much more office-based. He hangs around the water cooler and photocopier trying to chat up new recruits, boring them with lengthy stories of what it was like in the company before all these ridiculous emails stopped people actually talking, how he helped make it the multi-national it is today and how he believes in old-fashioned sales techniques and none of this brainstorming flipchart peer-assessment rubbish. Steve has a receding hairline, halitosis and haemorrhoids, and wears too much aftershave. He still thinks he is a pretty cool guy and that the 'young ladies' in the company will want to go for a drink with him and find out more (not about the haemorrhoids, obviously). He thinks they think he could help them get promoted...

LOVE EXPERIENCE:
Steve's ex-wife Joan and he were teenage sweethearts who married at 20. Steve would love to have an office romance and can get rather excited when in the presence of a pair of long legs attached to a short skirt.

He gets drunk at office parties. He once went for a meal with Valerie from Human Resources when she was between men from Accounts.

FAVOURITE FILMS:
Bond films (the ones with Sean Connery), Grease.

FAVOURITE MUSIC:
Love song compilations, Dire Straits and the Best of Classical set he bought from the Sunday papers

FASHION STYLE:
grey slip-ons, grey trousers, grey jacket (an unintentionally different grey) and statement tie (the Incredible Hunk design is the worst).

DANCE STYLE:
Steve is a John Travolta Dancer in the purest sense – he comes alive on the dance floor, while others just want to die... The arms, the legs, the head, the pointing, the pouting, the energy, the look on his face (and the look on everyone else's).

INTERESTS AND HOBBIES:
Fishing and the 19th hole (he's not that good on the first 18).

PETS:
He has two huge Koi fish in his pond at home.

BEST CHAT UP LINE:
'Young boys today have got no idea how to treat a lovely young lady like you.'

FANTASY LOVE LOCATION:
The stationery cupboard.

ANY DISTINGUISHING MARKS:
Beer belly and shiny head.

MOST ENDEARING HABIT:
Always brings you cups of coffee.

WORST HABIT:
Picking his nose during meetings and leaning too far over the watercooler.

PROS AND CONS
Steve is a nice enough guy but a bit of a worn (if not balding) retread in the tyre shop of life. He is keener on himself than anyone else is likely to be. He could be useful as a friend and ally at work but a relationship with him is not really to be advised. It took Joan a while to realise but Steve isn't the most exciting guy in town.

LOVE POTENTIAL:
No (unless you are desperate).

The Delivery Guy

The Delivery Guy is seen in offices at regular intervals during the day and early evening. He can also be spotted at speed on the road, deftly weaving between obstacles. His protective outer gear is usually black and leathery and he usually sports a helmet. He is a restless creature, always on the move, and he is very attractive to the female of the species.

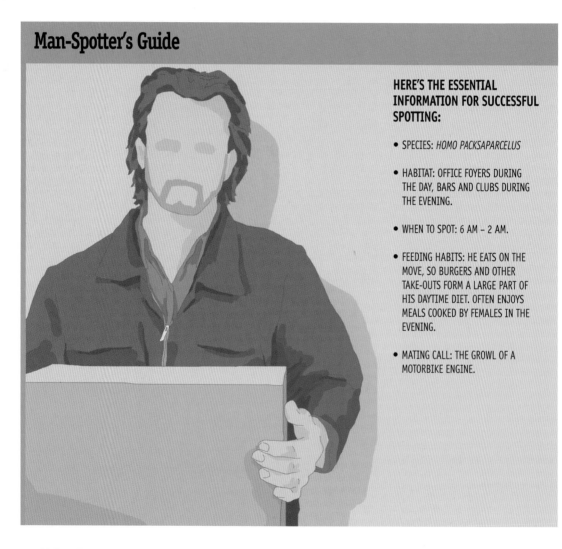

Man-Spotter's Guide

HERE'S THE ESSENTIAL INFORMATION FOR SUCCESSFUL SPOTTING:

- SPECIES: *HOMO PACKSAPARCELUS*

- HABITAT: OFFICE FOYERS DURING THE DAY, BARS AND CLUBS DURING THE EVENING.

- WHEN TO SPOT: 6 AM – 2 AM.

- FEEDING HABITS: HE EATS ON THE MOVE, SO BURGERS AND OTHER TAKE-OUTS FORM A LARGE PART OF HIS DAYTIME DIET. OFTEN ENJOYS MEALS COOKED BY FEMALES IN THE EVENING.

- MATING CALL: THE GROWL OF A MOTORBIKE ENGINE.

THE DELIVERY GUY

NAME:	Ric (aka The Hunk and The Parcel)
DATE OF BIRTH:	Not long enough ago (but does age really matter?)
OCCUPATION:	He delivers (boy, does he deliver)
ADDRESS:	No fixed abode (depends on his girlfriend of the month)

PERSONAL ATTRIBUTES:
Ric is seriously cute: C for cute, U for unbelievably cute, T for totally cute and E for every girl's dream of cute. He is fit in all senses of the word, too. Even the seriously ambitious, workaholic, never-smiles Head of Marketing wants to add him to her list of one-to-one staff assessments. He has the body of a Greek god, he is part-Italian and he is fluent in body language. He is all abs, no flab, with an irresistible little butt, slightly wavy, dark brown hair that hangs just over the collar of his nicely worn leather jacket, big, dark, soulful (come-to-bed – OK back to my place, then) eyes with lashes you couldn't even buy and a mouth that says 'Position vacant for girlfriend, apply here.' Ric always has a gentle sprinkling of stubble –just the right amount to be macho yet boyish in appeal. He may not have many academic qualifications and he will only make it into the boardroom when he delivers, but promotion in the bedroom is no problem. Ric is generous with his talents and happy to share his bodily possessions.

LOVE EXPERIENCE:
Ric's father was a scientist and taught his son the importance of doing thorough, repeated research before committing things to paper. Ric took him at his word and has been researching the relationship between him and women ever since and is a few years away from signing on the dotted line of a marriage certificate. Field studies are

going well and there is no shortage of candidates. He doesn't even have to advertise. He doesn't have much disposable income but is not embarrassed to let his girlfriends pay for the pleasure of a night out with him. He contributes in other ways. Women want to put him in their briefcase and take him home so they can study statistics in bed at night. Taking work home has never been more enjoyable.

FAVOURITE FILMS:
Tarantino, anything with James Dean in it.

FAVOURITE MUSIC:
Destiny's Child, 50 Cent.

FASHION STYLE:
Ric spends a good deal of his time in leathers. He looks good in them, but even better in denims and an abs-hugging T-shirt. He looks good in his birthday suit too, and his birthday seems to come around quite frequently.

DANCE STYLE:
Ric does the Pecs and Pelvis on the dance floor. He sees dancing as a vertical form of horizontal fun. He has rhythm, timing and all the right moves under his belt.

INTERESTS AND HOBBIES:
Gigs, clubs, bars, comedy venues, long walks in secluded forests, soccer.

PETS:
When he gets a place of his own or finds Mrs Right, Ric wants to get a snake called The Charmer.

BEST CHAT UP LINE:
'I think I have got a parcel for you'.

FANTASY LOVE LOCATION:
Secluded forests, leather jacket used as a blanket

ANY DISTINGUISHING MARKS:
Best butt in town.

MOST ENDEARING HABIT:
Makes you feel you are the only woman in the world.

WORST HABIT:
Forgets his wallet rather too often.

PROS AND CONS
Every girl needs a Ric in their past, present or future love portfolio. File him under R for research. In years to come, when you think back to a special moment and smile, it is probably because you are remembering that night with Ric.

LOVE POTENTIAL:
Yeeessssssss!

IT Nerd

The IT Nerd is becoming an increasingly common species. By default, at least one example of the sub-species *Geekus nerdicus professionalis* is to be found in every form of professional establishment that uses computers. IT Nerds permeate society as a whole and are not confined to urban environments, although they are slightly more common in towns and cities. Similar in appearance to *Geekus accountanti* (a dull and highly undistinguished species not covered in this book), they also congregate in large numbers in annual *United Nerdus* conventions.

Man-Spotter's Guide

HERE'S THE ESSENTIAL INFORMATION FOR SUCCESSFUL SPOTTING:

- SPECIES: *GEEKUS NERDICUS*

- HABITAT: FRESH-AIR-FEARING CREATURES, THEY HUDDLE INSIDE THEIR HOMES AND OFFICES AND RARELY VENTURE OUTDOORS.

- WHEN TO SPOT: MAY DEMONSTRATE OCCD (OBSESSIVE COMPUTER COMPULSIVE DISORDER) AND CAN BE SEEN IN FRONT OF THEIR MONITORS THROUGHOUT THE DAY AND NIGHT.

- FEEDING HABITS: GRAZES CONTINUALLY ON SANDWICHES, CRISPS AND CHOCOLATE BARS. DRINKS MAINLY COFFEE, AND ENJOYS LAPTOP MEALS.

- MATING CALL: ARE YOU ONLINE?

IT NERD

NAME:	Andy (aka Android, 'Andy-for-when-your-laptop-goes-down, Specky Tecky)
DATE OF BIRTH:	1979, the year the first Pac-man video game was sold in Japan
OCCUPATION:	Andrew in IT
ADDRESS:	Attic bedroom in his parents' semi-detached suburban house

PROFESSIONAL EXPERTISE:
Andrew lives in his own world. He is clever, with a brain that is a spaghetti junction of computer codes and a beyond-pale, thin-as-a-rail body that is a stranger to the sun, the sea, the swimming pool and other things beginning with 's'. He has zero social skills. He's the guy you call when your email goes down. He is no he-male, but, after just five minutes up close and personal with your PC's keyboard, Andrew will know which button to press to stimulate parts of your hard drive you've never reached. The only trouble is, you won't have a clue what he is talking about. Andrew might be able to speak fluent pc, but give him a living, breathing human being and he's in big trouble.

LOVE EXPERIENCE:
Andrew once smiled at girl waiting at No 19 bus stop, but apart from that he looks for love on internet chat lines. He is currently 'involved' with Tiffany who thinks he is a tall hip-hop DJ with a big rig and a Harley Davidson.

FAVOURITE FILMS:
Keanu Reeves and The Matrix – Andrew often fantasises that he is The One, fighting evil with reflexes faster than the speed of light.

FAVOURITE MUSIC:
Kraftwork and early Electronica.

FASHION STYLE:
In his head Andrew sports a long black leather coat and oh-so-cool wrap-around shades as he prowls the virtual world Keanu-style, but in reality his work attire is a shapeless shirt and a highly flammable tie, with shirt tails frequently making a bid for freedom over his belt in order to escape the close proximity of his less than savoury Y(oh, why?)-fronts. At weekends he might not even get out of his pyjamas. On the internet, nobody knows you're a skunk not a punk-hunk.

DANCE STYLE:
Hasn't really danced since an embarrassing incident at the school disco when he made the mistake of thinking he looked really cool playing 'air keyboard', but if forced, he's a Shy Shuffler. Sometimes he gets carried away and closes his eyes while he mouths the words.

INTERESTS AND HOBBIES:
Maintaining his website, tinkering with his computer, reading computer magazines, playing online computer games.

PETS AND PENCHANTS:
Andrew's low-maintenance pet is his constant and faithful companion. It doesn't need to have its claws clipped, its litter tray emptied or its system de-wormed because, no surprises, it's a virtual pet. Andrew has virtual penchants, too.

BEST CHAT UP LINE:
'I have got a huge hard drive. Let's hook up sometime.'

FANTASY LOVE LOCATION:
A sumptuous suite in a hotel in Tokyo or Silicone Valley with a state of the art computer set up and his and hers joysticks.

ANY DISTINGUISHING MARKS:
Huge thumbs from long hours playing his Game Boy, Bushbaby, myopic, squinting eyes, muscle-free body.

MOST ENDEARING HABIT:
Sorts your IT problems in seconds.

WORST HABIT:
Emails you all the time.

PROS AND CONS
Relationships with techno guys have their advantages. He can sort all your technical problems before you say 'loose connection' and fix anything with a lead, wire or plug. However, unless you come equipped with any of these, he may find connecting with you on an emotional level much trickier. He is more comfortable with love on the screen than trying to be a screen lover.

LOVE POTENTIAL:
No (sorry Andy).

The Jock

The Jock can be clearly identified by his height and bulk. Due to the bulge of his biceps, his arms are held out to the sides slightly as he walks, giving him an ape-like gait in extreme cases. Regardless of the weather, he can often be seen wearing a vest top or cut-away T-shirt that shows off his thick neck, muscular shoulders and back to best advantage. The Jock is a fairly common sighting in most towns and cities. He is narcissistic and preens in front of females and mirrors. He may also wear designer stubble designed to emphasise his masculinity.

Man-Spotter's Guide

HERE'S THE ESSENTIAL INFORMATION FOR SUCCESSFUL SPOTTING:

- SPECIES: *SEXTUS PACKUS MAXIMUS*

- HABITAT: THE GYM, THE FITNESS CLUB, SPORTS FIELD, WATCHING THE MATCH OR GAME.

- WHEN TO SPOT: 7 AM – LATE (IF THE MATCH OR GAME RUNS INTO EXTRA TIME).

- FEEDING HABITS: CARNIVORE – THREE BIG MEALS A DAY CONTAINING PLENTY OF PROTEIN, AND DIETARY SUPPLEMENTS TO BUILD THOSE MUSCLES. SNACKS AND CEREAL BARS AND SPORTS DRINKS. MAY ALSO TAKE BANNED SUBSTANCES PROVIDING HE DOESN'T THINK HE'LL BE TESTED FOR THEM.

- MATING CALL: FANCY CHECKING HOW HARD MY MUSCLES ARE?

THE JOCK

NAME:	Dom (aka The Dom Phenom)
DATE OF BIRTH:	1984
OCCUPATION:	Sporting hero and star athlete
ADDRESS:	New condo near the gym with his big bro Brett

PERSONAL ATTRIBUTES:
Meet one big, 6'6" rippling muscle that goes by the name of Dom. It starts at the neck and goes all the way down to the ankles, bulging, flexing, convex, concave, in all the right places. Dom is at the top of his form, his body is in a league of its own and his averages per game are way above human. Dom lives for sport. His athletic prowess is his personal trophy. If he could get a miniature version of himself, he would keep it on the shelf with all the other engraved shields, bowls, cups and trophies. Dom didn't get many A grades in exams, but he shattered all the records on record at college and makes more money than any of the guys who got to the top universities (yeah, so suck on that, guys). His finances are made to bulge even further through advertisements for his own personal line of asset-protecting sports gear, known as Jox in the Box. Dom is the Jock of Jocks. He bought his parents a new home and he loves his Mum. He has a big heart, an overdeveloped bank account and an underdeveloped interest in books, although he once took out a really cute librarian.

LOVE EXPERIENCE:
Dom broke lots of hearts as a teen. He is still breaking hearts now. He went out with every blonde cheerleader in the class, but he has matured since then and includes brunettes and red heads in his collection now. Dom is playing the field and scoring with his usual professional regularity and skill. Dom is nowhere near ready to settle down. There are too many girls out there whom he has yet to put in the back of the net. He needs new bedposts now there are so many notches on his old ones.

FAVOURITE FILMS:
Jerry Maguire, Tin Cup, Coach Carter, ones about sport.

FAVOURITE MUSIC:
Top 20 Cheerleader hits, national anthem, 'Simply The Best' by Tina Turner.

FASHION STYLE:
Dom wears great Hawaiian shorts, tight T-shirts saying 'I'm Your Man' and 'Don't window shop, try the goods on' and jeans that show every muscle movement. He likes to go topless when he can – to let his muscles and skin breathe.

DANCE STYLE:
Dom does the Muscle Hustle. He flexes his thigh muscles, moves from side to side (his usual style of walking) and sways, hands on hips. He whoops a lot.

INTERESTS AND HOBBIES:
Playing sport, watching sport, talking about sport, thinking about sport, dreaming about sport, taking chicks to matches.

PETS:
A rat called Dom Two.

BEST CHAT UP LINE:
'Hi, you're next.'

FANTASY LOVE LOCATION:
The locker room.

ANY DISTINGUISHING MARKS:
Pecs to die for and buns of steel.

MOST ENDEARING HABIT:
Remembers your name the next day.

WORST HABIT:
Forgets it again by the evening.

PROS AND CONS
Dom has a great physique and is a fantastic bit of Saturday night arm candy for a girl, but don't expect to see much of him after the weekend. Dom moves on. He has to score as many times as he can – that is what he is about.

LOVE POTENTIAL:
Yes (as long as you know the score).

The Artist

The artist is more easily identified by his bohemian behaviour rather than his plumage, although the latter is likely to reflect an 'alternative' lifestyle. You will rarely spot an artist in a suit – his plumage will more often be flowing or at least loosely fitted, mostly black in colour. The artist rises and retires late. You are unlikely to spot the artist on the high street. His haunts are the more obscure, yet-to-be-reported parts of the environment. His clothes are nuanced, tone-on-tone pre-loved chic.

Man-Spotter's Guide

HERE'S THE ESSENTIAL INFORMATION FOR SUCCESSFUL SPOTTING:

- SPECIES: *HOMO ARTI FARTI*

- HABITAT: STUDIOS, WORKSHOPS, PAINT-YOUR-OWN PLATE, OR ANY CREATIVE ENVIRONMENT, MAY ALSO BE SEEN STUDYING OTHER WORK IN GALLERIES, MUSEUMS, AND SO ON.

- WHEN TO SPOT: ANY TIME OF DAY OR NIGHT, DEPENDING UPON WHEN THE MUSE HAS STRUCK.

- FEEDING HABITS: ERRATIC. A SNACKER AND GRAZER OR INADVERTANT FASTER – THE ARTIST HAS HIGHER THINGS TO THINK OF AND WHILE WORKING MAY FORGET TO EAT COMPLETELY. LIKELY TO BE VEGETARIAN OR EVEN VEGAN.

- MATING CALL: THE SOUND OF A PAINTBRUSH ON CANVAS

THE ARTIST

NAME:	Lorenzo Darling (you couldn't make it up – but he might have)
DATE OF BIRTH:	Mid to late 60s
OCCUPATION:	Artist and bohemian
ADDRESS:	Basement flat in now trendy area

PERSONAL ATTRIBUTES:
Lorenzo has wanted to be an artist ever since he can remember. He was dyslexic at school, dreadful at maths, hopeless at sport but brilliant at art and deeply in love with the art teacher, Miss Teak (Veronica to her friends and Veronique after her sabbatical in Paris studying art therapy). Lorenzo is sensitive, thoughtful and prone to depression. He is 'dark, deep and sometimes difficult' according to his friends. He never has any money, but he gets life models for free so that helps. He is investigating selling his work on-line. He gets lots of inspiration at the 'artists' co-op café-studio' run by a friend, where he helps out for a bit of cash. He had an exhibition recently there and sold some stuff.

LOVE EXPERIENCE:
Lorenzo is a free spirit. He doesn't do traditional commitment. He does long-term liaisons, generally speaking. He doesn't really believe in marriage. It didn't work for his parents so why should it work for him? Art doesn't have boundaries so why should he? He spent some time living in a commune but it didn't work out – he had different life principles. Lorenzo dates his life models or models his life on dates, depending on the order of things.

ARTISTIC HERO:
Picasso.

FAVOURITE MUSIC:
The Velvet Undergound, Edith Piaf, Serge Gainsborough.

FAVOURITE FILMS:
Girl With Pearl Earring, Lost in Translation, anything with subtitles or set in Paris.

FASHION STYLE:
Lorenzo's fashion palette is mostly black, but he interrupts it with a sudden, surprising interjection of colour, like an orange scarf or a strip of violet silk draped around his neck with studied but artistic negligence. He wears corduroy in the winter and would wear more pure linen in the summer if he could afford it. Creases in clothes are de rigueur. They are the way clothes talk. The ladies at the charity shops put stuff aside for him.

DANCE STYLE:
Lorenzo does the Van Gogh For It – hand on one ear as if listening to himself in the studio. He sways slightly, a troubled, sometimes deeply troubled look upon his face, engrossed in the artistic expression that is dance.

INTERESTS AND HOBBIES:
Opening nights (free drinks and lots of luvvies), galleries, helping out with teaching hopeless amateur enthusiasts on expensive summer painting courses in Italy.

PETS:
A Siamese cat called Veronique and a terrier called Ralphie who love each other.

BEST CHAT UP LINE:
'You have great cheeks' and 'Ever thought of being a life-drawing model?'

FANTASY LOVE LOCATION:
Big studio in Montmartre, light streaming in, Edith Piaf singing in the background, glass of Beaujolais in one hand, big brush in the other.

ANY DISTINGUISHING MARKS:
Agonised suffering-artist expression.

MOST ENDEARING HABIT:
Tells you that you are his greatest muse.

WORST HABIT:
Pays like Van Gogh (i.e. Dutch)

PROS AND CONS
Lorenzo is unreliable on the love stakes. He is both afraid of and doesn't really believe in commitment. He is more of a love for free and freedom in love kind of guy. But Lorenzo is interesting and can talk for hours about post-modernism. If you like long evenings in dark bars talking about art imitating life and life imitating art, this is your guy.

LOVE POTENTIAL:
Worth having a brush with a bohemian at least once in your life.

The Media Guy

The Media Guy is an unusually rare species, only spotted in large towns and cities with film, TV, publicity or press links. This is the natural habitat of the Media Guy, whose networking instincts are very strong. He therefore tends to be found in small herds at watering holes such as trendy bars and pubs, exchanging contacts and phone numbers. Relatively hard to spot, look for clothing that is self-consciously cool, dark glasses and designer stubble. Bright ties or socks are often give-away signs, together with a large expensive watch. Rarely separated from his cell phone.

Man-Spotter's Guide

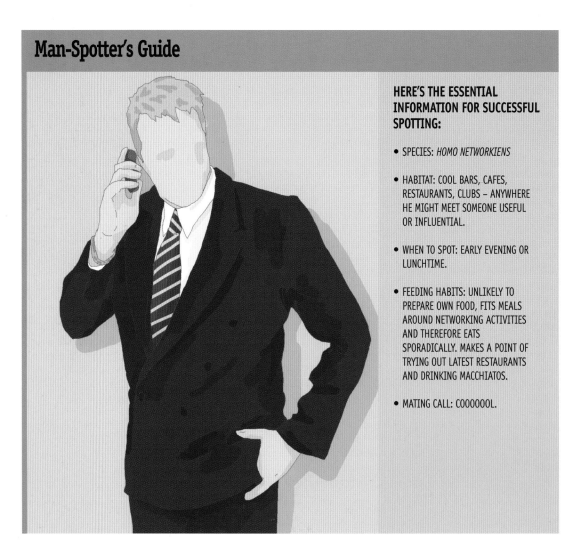

HERE'S THE ESSENTIAL INFORMATION FOR SUCCESSFUL SPOTTING:

- SPECIES: *HOMO NETWORKIENS*

- HABITAT: COOL BARS, CAFES, RESTAURANTS, CLUBS – ANYWHERE HE MIGHT MEET SOMEONE USEFUL OR INFLUENTIAL.

- WHEN TO SPOT: EARLY EVENING OR LUNCHTIME.

- FEEDING HABITS: UNLIKELY TO PREPARE OWN FOOD, FITS MEALS AROUND NETWORKING ACTIVITIES AND THEREFORE EATS SPORADICALLY. MAKES A POINT OF TRYING OUT LATEST RESTAURANTS AND DRINKING MACCHIATOS.

- MATING CALL: COOOOOOL.

THE MEDIA GUY

NAME:	Joshua (aka JJ, Posh-Josh)
DATE OF BIRTH:	Very, very late 70s
OCCUPATION:	Account Executive in an internationally renowned ad agency
ADDRESS:	Cool, minimalist, downtown bachelor pad

PERSONAL ATTRIBUTES:
Josh is a workaholic. He gets a cab from the gym to his office at ABAB, D&C (who are just about to be taken over by F & F) around 7.30am to check his emails, liaise with overseas subsidiaries and chat up the night-shift secretaries (they are so tired they succumb more easily). He buys a triple strength macchiato en route and a few energy drinks to keep him going during the day. He spends a few moments in the men's washroom (the one without the security camera) before hitting his desk and calling the florist to deliver 12 red roses to his latest girlfriend whom he had to stand up the night before when a meeting came up last minute with Boring Belinda in PR. Josh is good looking in a slightly tired, wrinkles-just-appearing-around-his-eyes kind of way. He is fit (he should be, he has a very expensive personal trainer) and tanned (yeah, well, he goes skiing for the weekend and hits Barbados regularly). He leaves the office around 8pm most nights. He is glued to his cell phone day and night and has half a dozen different email addresses.

LOVE EXPERIENCE:
Josh has had three or four serious relationships and more than a handful of flings. He is a smooth-talker and knows all the right restaurants and bars and is a member of a couple of exclusive clubs, where he impresses his often much younger girlfriends. He goes on spa holidays and enjoyed a particularly relaxing one in Malaysia recently. Josh is a chain romancer. He can't leave one girl until her successor has been targeted. He has never had his heart broken.

FAVOURITE FILMS:
Wall Street, Foreign films, anything with subtitles.

FAVOURITE MUSIC:
Rolling Stones, Miles Davis, Coldplay.

FASHION STYLE:
Josh spends big money on designer suits and handmade shirts and shoes. He had a couple of suits made in Bangkok only this year, in fact. He has around 100 ties, silk pyjamas (and silk sheets actually...), designer boxers, braces in loud colours and, of course, the latest in sports gear and shoes. His casual wear is just a little bit young for him. He wears bracelets.

DANCE STYLE:
Josh is a bit of a Gyrater on the dance floor and when he has downed too many vodkas and energy drinks he is more of a Gyrattitude. His arms and hands seem to have a career of their own and his pelvis does overtime and out-of-time.

INTERESTS AND HOBBIES:
Flashy cars, luxury holidays, massages, recreational activities, weekends away in expensive hotels in the country, off-piste and heli-skiing, drinking clubs, work trips to foreign capitals.

PETS:
His housekeeper looks after his tropical fish, Jaws.

BEST CHAT UP LINE:
'You look a million dollars - exactly the amount in my bank account...'

FANTASY LOVE LOCATION:
Luxury tropical resort, Pina Coladas on tap, freshly plucked mangoes, private pool...

ANY DISTINGUISHING MARKS:
Permanent tan.

MOST ENDEARING HABIT:
Has an account at Jimmy Choo.

WORST HABIT:
Never turns off his cell phone.

PROS AND CONS
Josh is a dangerous catch. It will take a seriously strong woman to convince him to give up serial romancing and commit to her. He is driven by his desire for corporate success, serious money, indulgent holidays, fast women and a Porsche (or a fast car and a woman called Porsche). Josh lives for the moment. Tomorrow is just a day when something better might come along. He excels at the above-the-line promotions at work. Up to you to check out if the below-the-line skills are worth it.

LOVE POTENTIAL:
Yes (if you know what you are doing).

The Rock Star

The Rock Star has a tendency to be vain and often sports showy plumage in order to be noticed by adoring fans/potential mates. He enjoys performing and strutting about the stage, striking poses or punching his fist in the air. His hair can be very long and may be tied into a ponytail when not performing. He may have piercings and other body markings (e.g. tattoos) and can be of any height; he is often slim to skinny. The less well-off sub-species may have a day job such as driving a van or working as a mechanic. The Rock Star is fairly uncommon and a sighting therefore usually generates considerable interest.

Man-Spotter's Guide

HERE'S THE ESSENTIAL INFORMATION FOR SUCCESSFUL SPOTTING:

- SPECIES: *HOMO ROCKNROLLUS*

- HABITAT: MUSIC VENUES, BARS, ANYWHERE WITH A STAGE AND AN ELECTRICAL SOCKET INTO WHICH HE CAN PLUG HIS GUITAR.

- WHEN TO SPOT: GENERALLY SEMI-NOCTURNAL, 8 PM – 12 PM, EXCEPT AT FESTIVALS WHEN MAY BE SIGHTED ANYTIME FROM 10 AM ONWARDS IF IN UNKNOWN-BAND WARM-UP SLOT.

- FEEDING HABITS: LIKELY TO BE VEGETARIAN AND EAT A SURPRISINGLY HEALTHY DIET IN AN EFFORT TO MAKE UP FOR ALCOHOL AND NICOTINE ABUSE.

- MATING CALL: HEAVILY AMPLIFIED SCREAM.

THE ROCK STAR

NAME:	Jake (aka King Jay, Jay Boy, the Axe Man)
DATE OF BIRTH:	1981, the year Metallica were formed in Los Angeles
OCCUPATION:	Driver for a frozen food company by day, rock 'star' by night
ADDRESS:	The 'Purple Pad'

PROFESSIONAL EXPERTISE:
Jake thinks his voice will be his fortune. A studious combination of gravel and grit, it has the quality of a cat being dragged away from a mouse by its tail when rising to a crescendo to hit the high notes of the heavy metal scream. Jake's family is solidly middle class – Dad's a stockbroker and his brother a wine merchant – but you wouldn't know it from Jake's street accent, which he acquired some time between his last year at boarding school and first year at uni. After searching for his musical direction experimenting with different bands – Blazin' Yoof (hip-hop), Avallon (grunge), Elysian Fields (art house) – during the second year of his art foundation course he finally joined straightforward, no-nonsense rockers and heavy metal wannabes Valhalla and promptly dropped out. Their music is unsubtle, unvaried and unspeakably loud.

LOVE EXPERIENCE:
Heavily into rock chicks, he's expert at zipping two sleeping bags together at festivals.

FAVOURITE FILMS:
Spinal Tap.

FAVOURITE SONG/SINGER:
Light My Fire (Jim Morrison is a god).

FASHION STYLE:
Wasted with a bony chest and rock-star pallor, Jake is not yet old enough to have that Keith Richard I've-done-it-all look, but he's doing his best to cultivate it. But don't be totally taken in by the black leather trousers, studded leather belt slung low on his hips, flowery shirt rolled up to the elbows revealing tattoo tigers rampant on his skinny forearms... Jake is very vain about his hair. No 'wash-n' go' kinda guy, he spends hours shampooing and conditioning it every day leaving it to dry naturally in a deliberate tangle.

DANCE STYLE:
Legs stiff and splayed, head down, hair falling around his face, eyes closed, Jake is in riff heaven when playing air guitar.

INTERESTS AND HOBBIES:
Music of course, attending gigs, switching his amp up to 11 and blasting the neighbours out.

PETS:
In an apartment as noisy as the 'Purple Pad', the animal welfare officer would be round in a flash to remove the sensitive ears of a dog or cat out of harm's way, so Jake and his flatmate Dirk have settled for a goldfish called Soundbite, who rather enjoys the tickling sensation caused by the decibel induced waves that ripple through his bowl during jamming sessions.

BEST CHAT UP LINE:
'Allo darlin'.

FANTASY LOVE LOCATION:
A teepee on a warm summer's night at a rock festival and a crate of beer but clean latrines. (Jake lives in hope, although festivals and fragrant toilets are generally mutually exclusive.)

ANY DISTINGUISHING MARKS:
Slightly deaf. Well, there's a surprise.

MOST ENDEARING HABIT:
Remembers his name the next day.

WORST HABIT:
Thinks every woman is called Darlin'.

PROS AND CONS
Once you get past the studded belt, leather trousers and tousled hair, you might be surprised to find Jake's feminine side is not far from the surface. He also has beautiful manners that several years with Dirk have not yet been able to eradicate. So, if you can put up with his obsessive interest in noise, he's a good bet for a fun time and will impress your more conventional friends. The only drawback is Dirk, so if you can manage to date Jake, insist on going back to your place.

LOVE POTENTIAL:
Yeah, man, go for it.

The Doctor

Despite being fairly common in both town and country – although younger members of the species gravitate towards urban environments – the doctor can be hard to spot away from his surgery, which is his natural habitat. He may be marked out by his confident and rather superior air. However, if in doubt, try flushing him out by having a friend pretend to be ill and asking loudly, 'Is there a doctor in the house?' The Hippocratic oath should ensure that this highly prized species loses his inhibitions and whips out his stethoscope right away.

Man-Spotter's Guide

HERE'S THE ESSENTIAL INFORMATION FOR SUCCESSFUL SPOTTING:

- SPECIES: *HOMO MEDICANS (COATI BIANCHI)*

- HABITAT: SURGERIES, HOSPITALS, CLINICS AND OTHER MEDICAL ENVIRONMENTS.

- WHEN TO SPOT: SHIFT WORK, PAGERS AND CALL-OUTS ENSURE THAT HE CAN BE SPOTTED ANY TIME OF DAY, ANY DAY OF THE YEAR.

- FEEDING HABITS: DESPITE INTIMATE KNOWLEDGE OF THE CORRECT DIETARY REQUIREMENTS FOR HIS SPECIES, HE MAY SMOKE AND DRINK TO EXCESS.

- MATING CALL: BEEP, BEEP, BEEP.

THE DOCTOR

NAME:	Guy London (aka The Face and Take it Away, London...)
DATE OF BIRTH:	Hard to tell
OCCUPATION:	Medical expert
ADDRESS:	A brand new apartment overlooking a marina

PROFESSIONAL EXPERTISE:
Skilful cosmetic surgeon to the rich and famous, thanks to his ability to hold back the years without any of the usual drawbacks (frozen foreheads, trout lips, guys having to shave behind their ears, girls with disproportionate and alarmingly pert attributes), he has achieved god-like status among his patients. His treatment is known as 'Take it Away, London' (you simply must use him, darling).

LOVE EXPERIENCE:
Can a man have too much experience? If so, Guy is well on his way to achieving it. With his languid half-swallowed, suave though slightly swaggering manner, he is a babe magnet. A relationship with Guy will take years off you.

FAVOURITE FILMS:
Face Off.

FAVOURITE SONG/SINGER:
'Holding Back the Years' by Simply Red.

FASHION STYLE:
ER meets Mr Big. At work he sports a sparkling white coat devoid of bodily fluids – it's the nurses who do all the dirty work while Guy inspects the occasional breast or draws lines over 'before' and 'after' identikit photos prior to wielding the scalpel. A stethoscope dangles nonchalantly but rather redundantly around his neck. Beneath his white coat, the badge of his trade, lies a monogrammed shirt and tie and Italian-cut suit. In the evenings he takes a taxi back to his bachelor apartment where he showers and changes into smart-casual chinos, polo shirt and loafers with a sweater draped over his shoulders.

DANCE STYLE:
Guy doesn't waste energy on needless dance moves and other histrionics. He looks good and moves well, putting in just the right amount of effort to get the girl.

INTERESTS AND HOBBIES:
Tinkering on his yacht, which so far has not yet left its mooring, weekends with friends at house parties, fine wine, the theatre, luxury holidays.

PETS AND PENCHANTS:
Guy keeps his dog, Achilles, at his parents' house in the country and manages to get down there about once every few months. Achilles remains slavishly faithful to his master, despite his infrequent visits.

BEST CHAT UP LINE:
'You're certainly a cut above the rest, babe.'

FANTASY LOVE LOCATION:
Rome, Verona or Boston for the weekend – a little sight-seeing, a romantic dinner for two or an evening at the opera, after which he and his girlfriend retire to sample the dolce vita in their sumptuous hotel suite, all gold drapes, marble plush carpet and pristine white cotton sheets.

ANY DISTINGUISHING MARKS:
A steady hand, which is just as well because in his line of work he certainly needs one.

MOST ENDEARING HABIT:
Gazes into your eyes.

WORST HABIT:
Gazes into your eyes... and says 'you really should get rid of those bags.'

PROS AND CONS:
A good bet if you like a man who is attentive, confident in all situations and will take you on fantastic holidays. True, he is a little pleased with himself, but given the pros, perhaps this is something you can overlook for a while? As for the downside, as he gazes into your eyes and you wonder if he is noticing those bags, crow's feet and frown lines, it can be a little off-putting. And you may prefer to get undressed in the dark.

LOVE POTENTIAL:
Yes (hang in there until you get a new face for free).

The Millionaire

The Millionaire is an uncommon species and confirmed sightings are therefore rare and highly prized. If you are lucky enough to spot a Millionaire, record the location and circumstances immediately and if possible exchange phone numbers. The Millionaire's plumage is always expensive, but it may not be in the best possible taste. Often a workaholic, the Millionaire is often seen with his mobile phone glued to his ear doing deals, buying and selling, or sacking more lowly members of the male species.

Man-Spotter's Guide

HERE'S THE ESSENTIAL INFORMATION FOR SUCCESSFUL SPOTTING:

- SPECIES: *DOLLARUS MAXIMUS*

- HABITAT: THE MILLIONAIRE IS MIGRATORY, BUT IS USUALLY FOUND IN AN URBAN ENVIRONMENT. MAY ALSO BE SEEN IN AN EXPENSIVE FOREIGN SEASIDE LOCATION, ON A YACHT, OR CLIMBING INTO A PRIVATE JET OR HELICOPTER.

- WHEN TO SPOT: HIGHLY UNPREDICTABLE IN HIS MOVEMENTS.

- FEEDING HABITS: TENDS TO BE CARNIVOROUS, BUT CAN BE VEGETARIAN, FEEDS ONLY AT EXPENSIVE, QUALITY ESTABLISHMENTS.

- MATING CALL: BUY, BUY, BUY; SELL, SELL, SELL.

THE MILLIONAIRE

NAME:	Wayne Dodge (aka Wayne-Likes-a-Million-Dollars, Dodge Dollar)
DATE OF BIRTH:	3.5 x 10 years-old and millions-rich
OCCUPATION:	Businessman, wheeler 'n' dealer, ducker 'n' diver, shaker 'n' mover
ADDRESS:	Smart bachelor penthouse in a new block overlooking the river

PROFESSIONAL EXPERTISE:
In Wayne's world money talks, in fact it positively shouts, yells and screams. Wayne is a sales supremo with a degree from the University of The Street, who could sell a telescope to a blind man. He is very pleased with himself. A self-made man, he left school at 16 with two qualifications – one in survival techniques and one in creative accounting. If a street vendor sells 200 DVD players at 70% profit, but has to give a 20% cut on 150 of them to his supplier and pay 5% of his overall profit minus hidden costs for his market stall pitch, how much profit does he make? Wayne can do sums like that in his head in a flash.

LOVE EXPERIENCE:
A string of lovely ladies named after alcoholic drinks (Martini, Bianca, Chardonnay, Chartreuse and Cointreau) have been at his side, although not for long. Wayne is a shaker and a mover. He shakes off one girl after the other and moves on quickly. He is an old-fashioned guy, who prides himself on treating his women well. He pays for everything, including expensive meals, extravagant gifts, flowers, exotic holidays, in return for which the lady in question says and wears as little as possible but very much looks the part on his arm.

FAVOURITE FILMS:
Oceans 11 – though he prefers the 1960s version with Frank, Sammy, Deano and the boys.

FAVOURITE SONG/SINGER:
Frank he's the man Sinatra and Barry White to please the ladies and get them in the mood for lurve.

FASHION STYLE:
Labels, labels, labels. Wayne likes them and also prides himself on his bespoke sharp suits from his astronomically expensive tailor. He shaves close twice a day and keeps his hair slicked down. When he smiles, the hint of a gold tooth is just visible, while there's even more gold glinting in his bracelet, cufflinks and in the large ring on his pinkie. The 'bling tone' on his mobile is 'Money, money, money'. When negotiations get heated he takes off his jacket to reveal blood-red braces – ping them at your peril. You don't need to ask his PA if 'Wayne's in the building', you can tell from the smell of pungent and expensive aftershave that hangs in the air after Wayne has passed by.

DANCE STYLE:
The hustle of course, clubs being his natural hunting ground.

INTERESTS AND HOBBIES:
Cuban cigars, casinos, marlin fishing off Florida Keys, fast cars, buying new houses for his mum, and saunas.

PETS AND PENCHANTS:
There's no time in Wayne's life for pets just now, but he does own two racehorses called Here's Doping and An Arm and a Leg.

BEST CHAT UP LINE:
'Let me whisk you away to paradise'.

FANTASY LOVE LOCATION:
Somewhere hot and exotic where he can top up his tan, surrounded by bikini babes, and where the local language is money. Rio, Barbados, Vegas, Mauritius...

ANY DISTINGUISHING MARKS:
A small scar on his lip from a teenage fight with the guy on the next stall over pitch, wears it with pride and makes him look kinda sexy, teeth whiter than Tom's (that's Cruise not Thumb) after months in the orthodontist's chair, now named after him.

MOST ENDEARING HABIT:
Giving you diamonds at Christmas, on your birthday, on Tuesdays...

WORST HABIT:
Thinks he can buy anything – including you.

PROS AND CONS
Wayne is a good bet (literally) if you go in with your eyes open and your kitten heels on the right foot. He will spoil you, shower you with flowers and jewels, take you to Paris shopping and to lots of parties and opening nights. You will feel a million dollars, again literally, but he will never introduce you to his mum.

LOVE POTENTIAL:
Yes (for temporary fun).

The Fireman

The fireman's uniform marks him out as an important male species, performing a highly valuable function in society. He is common in all major towns and cities, but is less frequently seen in small village locations. It is, however, virtually impossible to spot an off-duty fireman. Out of uniform his plumage varies a great deal, making it hard to distinguish him from many other male species. Physically, a fireman is unlikely to be fat and is generally in good shape – adding to his high-level status.

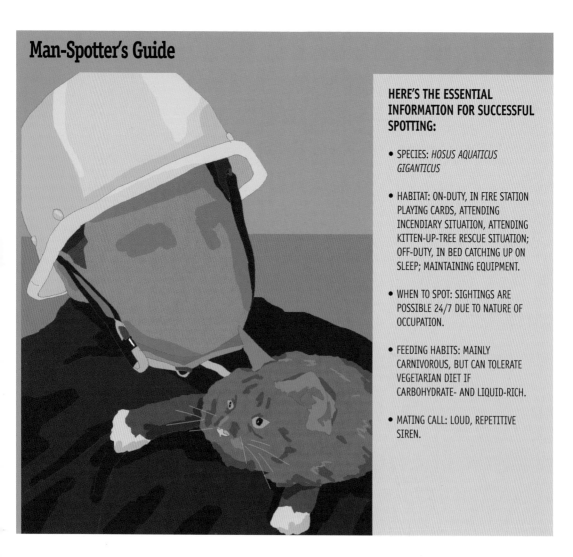

Man-Spotter's Guide

HERE'S THE ESSENTIAL INFORMATION FOR SUCCESSFUL SPOTTING:

- SPECIES: *HOSUS AQUATICUS GIGANTICUS*

- HABITAT: ON-DUTY, IN FIRE STATION PLAYING CARDS, ATTENDING INCENDIARY SITUATION, ATTENDING KITTEN-UP-TREE RESCUE SITUATION; OFF-DUTY, IN BED CATCHING UP ON SLEEP; MAINTAINING EQUIPMENT.

- WHEN TO SPOT: SIGHTINGS ARE POSSIBLE 24/7 DUE TO NATURE OF OCCUPATION.

- FEEDING HABITS: MAINLY CARNIVOROUS, BUT CAN TOLERATE VEGETARIAN DIET IF CARBOHYDRATE- AND LIQUID-RICH.

- MATING CALL: LOUD, REPETITIVE SIREN.

THE FIREMAN

NAME:	Joey (aka The Hose, Hosé, U-Can-Put-My-Fire-Out-Anytime)
DATE OF BIRTH:	Aquarius (the water sign...), 80s vintage
OCCUPATION:	Fireman and all-round hunk and hero
ADDRESS:	Suburban two-bed starter home.

PROFESSIONAL EXPERTISE:
Joey is a Can-Do, Fix-It, Have-a-go Hero. He rescues kittens from trees, heads from railings, damsels from distress (cue swoon...). And on top of everything else, he puts fires out.

LOVE EXPERIENCE:
Three steady girlfriends, one childhood sweetheart (who used to do impressions of a kitten up a tree so that Jack could rescue her) and a desperate housewife.

FAVOURITE FILMS:
Backdraft, anything with Sharon Stone, Clint Eastwood

FAVOURITE SONG/SINGER:
The theme tune to London's Burning.

FASHION STYLE:
Jack looks great in uniform, although with breathing apparatus he looks and sounds like Darth Vader, but when he's off duty he likes to keep it simple. He doesn't really pay much attention, unlike most of the women he knows, who think he looks hotter than hell in his scuffed jeans and T-shirt or chunky sweater. Sets hearts alight when he sports his dark suit, cheeks freshly shaved and steel butt at a jaunty angle for the fireman's ball.

DANCE STYLE:
More of a Bar Tapper, Joey spends most of the time with a beer in hand and only dances (very self-consciously) when he wants to get the girl.

INTERESTS AND HOBBIES:
Fixing his motorbike, scuba diving, soccer with the guys, a little pool to help him wind down after his shift, charity runs, looking after women on their own.

PETS AND PENCHANTS:
Would like to get a dog, but worried about leaving it alone in the house all day, so opted for a lower-maintenance type of pet that keeps his pillow warm – a cat that he got from the rescue centre (how sweet).

BEST CHAT UP LINE:
'Should we go back to your place just to check you turned the gas off?' 'Fancy coming back to do some maintenance on the pole back at the station?'

FANTASY LOVE LOCATION:
Scuba-diving in the Indian Ocean – he is very comfortable in a watery environment and good at heavy breathing.

ANY DISTINGUISHING MARKS:
'Asbestos hands' – most men can't pick up hot plates in the kitchen the way women can, but Jack's hands have been toughened up, the hard way.

MOST ENDEARING HABIT:
Wears his uniform in bed.

WORST HABIT:
Won't allow naked flames (including candles) in the house.

PROS AND CONS:
After having put in a good deal of overtime, Joey finally got himself on the property ladder last year (makes a change from the one on his fire engine), but he hasn't got used to going down the stairs yet, as opposed to sliding down a pole or climbing out of a window. Joey is a cool guy who can take the heat. He is handsome, looks great in and out of his uniform, saves lives for a living and knows what to do with a hose when things get hot. He is active, fit, sporty, attractive, popular, caring, brave, just macho enough without being too macho... what are you waiting for – the bells and sirens? Joey gets the girls for a good reason. Have fun finding out what it is.

LOVE POTENTIAL:
Yes! Yes! Yes!

The Construction Worker

The construction worker is a male species common to most urban environments. Easily identifiable by his hard hat – which is normally yellow in colour but sometimes white or fluorescent orange – he is an outdoor man of all seasons. Frequently shirtless throughout the warmer months, he can sport a deep tan from early spring through to late autumn, and older specimens often look weather-beaten. He may flaunt his rear in an unpleasant manner known as 'builder's bottom', but will attempt to appear unaware of this obvious display tactic.

Man-Spotter's Guide

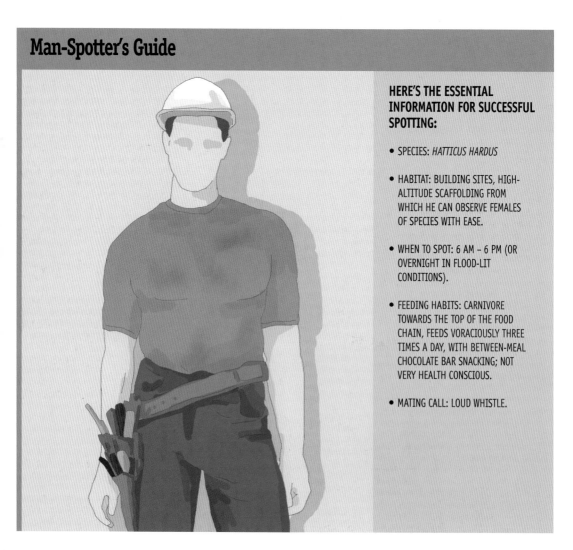

HERE'S THE ESSENTIAL INFORMATION FOR SUCCESSFUL SPOTTING:

- SPECIES: *HATTICUS HARDUS*

- HABITAT: BUILDING SITES, HIGH-ALTITUDE SCAFFOLDING FROM WHICH HE CAN OBSERVE FEMALES OF SPECIES WITH EASE.

- WHEN TO SPOT: 6 AM – 6 PM (OR OVERNIGHT IN FLOOD-LIT CONDITIONS).

- FEEDING HABITS: CARNIVORE TOWARDS THE TOP OF THE FOOD CHAIN, FEEDS VORACIOUSLY THREE TIMES A DAY, WITH BETWEEN-MEAL CHOCOLATE BAR SNACKING; NOT VERY HEALTH CONSCIOUS.

- MATING CALL: LOUD WHISTLE.

THE CONSTRUCTION WORKER

NAME:	Dan (aka Dan The Man, Can-Do Dan, but not Dictionary Dan)
DATE OF BIRTH:	1981
OCCUPATION:	Construction worker, He-man, hard-hat guy
ADDRESS:	Caravan on site at the moment

PROFESSIONAL EXPERTISE:
You name it, Dan can build it. Dan can erect anything from scaffolding to skyscrapers. Solid, predictable and reliable (Dan, not the scaffolding). Dan is more brawn than brain. He is no intellectual.

LOVE EXPERIENCE:
Less than you would think judging by his bulging muscles and tanned torso and six-pack, but Dan doesn't really have a way with words. He can make bricks into walls but not words into sentences. He is happy to whistle at females from the safety of his scaffolding and shout things like 'Nice smile' or 'Cor, phwoar, wow, look at the **** on that chick.' But smooth-talking isn't his style. Dan is no intellectual – he's more bungalow than multi-storeyed on the personality front, too. He tried speed dating but couldn't think of anything to say.

FAVOURITE FILMS:
Action movies, such as Die Hard and Cliff Hanger. Likes Bruce Willis.

FAVOURITE SONG/SINGER:
Kylie, he loves that pert, petite, coy but come-hither look.

FASHION STYLE:
Jeans and a white T-shirt, jeans and a logo T-shirt, jeans and a dirty T-shirt. That is Dan's fashion statement. Brick dust, tools and a flash of builder's butt are added extras. Doc Marten's are de rigueur this season.

DANCE STYLE:
Dan doesn't do dancing – that's that, full stop. Dan doesn't go to clubs or anywhere where there is the remotest possibility of dancing, except for family weddings when he is dragged onto the floor by his crazy cousin Cath whose boyfriend Doug has a bad back. Dan is a Stomper (think Action Man auditions for Riverdance).

INTERESTS AND HOBBIES:
Drinking with his mates, watching sport, and reading lads' mags.

PETS AND PENCHANTS:
No pets because you couldn't swing a cat in a caravan, but if he could have anything he wanted it would be a fine black stallion with which to round up his herd of cattle at the OK Corral Ranch in Marlborough Country.

BEST CHAT UP LINE:
'If I knew the alphabet I would put U and I together.'

FANTASY LOVE LOCATION:
A log cabin in the Midwest where men can be men and ladies can be ladies (especially if they are Kylie-sized).

ANY DISTINGUISHING MARKS:
With all those scars from the construction sites where do you start? Well you could begin with the dent in his leg that he got when helping his dad build the garden wall at the age of eight...

MOST ENDEARING HABIT:
Offers to check your plumbing for free.

WORST HABIT:
Wants you to change your name to Kylie.

PROS AND CONS:
Unless you have a building project in mind or a home in need of serious DIY work, Dan has more cons going for him than pros (not literally...). He is a constructing male rather than a de-constructed one and would be hard work if you are looking for a soul mate unless you are Babs the Builder yourself and more into rendering walls than romantic walks, hammering in nails rather than interesting tales and have hammers and drills in your toolbox, instead of kitten heels and vitamin pills.

LOVE POTENTIAL:
None (unless you've got a renovation project on the go).

Tools & Techniques

MANagement
Women need to manage men in just about every room in the house. Read on to learn some new and improved home management tactics.

Never Too Late
They say you can't teach an old dog new tricks, but what do they know? Use these new tricks – and don't date old dogs.

Learn to Flirt
Flirting has been around since Mr Neanderthal dated Miss Neanderthal. (He may even have tried his luck with Miss Cro-Magnon, but she was way out of his league.)

'Behind every successful man is a woman with a great toolbox'
VANESSA BYRNE, STRATEGIST, 2005

Perseverence is Key
Give a woman time, patience, determination and the right tools, and she will make a Mr Good Deal out of almost anything.

No MANopoly on tools

Some men just love their toolboxes (no, not that one!), full of shiny instruments of different sizes, application and efficiency. Sounds familiar? Like men, some of the items are more useful and well made than others. Some of men's toolboxes remain virginal, untouched, their packaging intact, their contents rather admired from afar. But should men have the monopoly on toolboxes? Are they just one more manopoly? Girls need tools, implements, indeed an entire range of arms, armoury and ammo to deal with the guys in their lives. Women have to do the physical stuff, too, like putting right and finishing off household jobs embarked upon and then abandoned, or simply ignored, by their men folk. Women can do plumbing, building, fixing, mending, painting, stripping (both sorts) so they know their way around a toolbox alright.

However, a very different kind of toolbox comes in very handy from time to time. Let's call it the Girl's Essential Toolbox. It is one of those really posh ones, with three layers, each one endowed with a specific purpose. The top layer contains all the tools you need to sort your guy out in the home. With these vital household management implements you will be able to get more help around the home. The middle layer contains practical advice on how to help your guy out when he is stressed, with its choice of de-stress mechanisms. If your man is a stress-head, then you will be too, so it works for both of you. The bottom layer, the secret, hidden compartment, contains the nitty-gritty, let's-get-down-to-basics tools – the ones the guys don't need to know about. This is the S&S and P&P drawer. Don't worry, there's nothing too naughty inside. The tools are more 21st-century Jane Austen than anything more daring. Seduction and Sensuality, Persuasion and Passion – this layer contains the all-important Keep-Your-Guy-Guessing pack. It's at the back of the book for ease of reference; it comes last but is extremely important, and women will know about that. Keep the book at hand – you might need to dip into it at any time. It is full of things a girl might need in one of life's many little emergencies.

It's all about control and direction. Men generally like to be in control, women frequently are; men often don't realise and women tend not to make it obvious. Let your guy think he is at the helm, respected commander of the boat taking you towards your ultimate destination, while you are gently steering him along the right course and in control of the speed of progress. Who said women were no good at navigating? They don't need maps for this kind of journey; they use instinct, landmarks and subtle pointers to keep guys on the right track and pointing in the right direction. Men sometimes need help at the helm but don't want either to admit it or ask for it. That shouldn't stop you giving him a hand with keeping the upper one. Read on...

Try answering the questions opposite and then try your hand using the hints and tips in the toolbox for handling your man in the home and in the bedroom. Learn how to help de-stress him and keep him calm when life gets on top of him, and then discover how to get your guy all excited again. In the meantime, he can give the bedroom a quick dust and vacuum. And if all this man management business gets on top of you, turn to page 142 and enjoy a spot of reward or revenge with the Voodoodle.

PETER PERFECT

Perfection only comes with practice. With your help, Peter will learn to practise perfection.

Man About the House

It's time to ask yourself a few questions about you and your man. You might not like all the answers but don't despair, help is at hand. Just dip into the Girl's Essential Toolbox.

LEFT TO HIS OWN DEVICES HOW OFTEN WOULD YOUR GUY CHANGE THE SHEETS?

A) ONCE IN A BLUE MOON
B) ONCE YOU REFUSED TO SLEEP IN THEM
C) ONCE A WEEK
D) ONCE A FORTNIGHT
E) ONCE HIS TEAM WON THE CHAMPIONSHIP
   (HE'S SUPERSTITIOUS...)

HOW FREQUENTLY DOES YOUR GUY OFFER TO HELP WTH THE VACUUMING?

A) REGULARLY
B) NEVER
C) IF HIS MOTHER IS COMING TO STAY
D) RARELY
E) WHENEVER YOU ASK

DO YOU THINK HOUSEWORK CAN MAKE A MAN SEXY?

A) DEFINITELY
B) SORT OF
C) NO
D) NEED MORE EXPLANATION (SEE PAGE 138)
E) HUH?

HOW OFTEN IS YOUR GUY TOO STRESSED TO 'GO UPSTAIRS'?

A) OFTEN
B) NEVER
C) FROM TIME TO TIME
D) NEVER ON HOLIDAY
E) NOT AS OFTEN AS YOU WOULD LIKE

IS YOUR MAN BAD TEMPERED AND STRESSED WHEN HE GETS BACK FROM WORK?

A) SOMETIMES
B) REGULARLY
C) ALL THE TIME
D) NEVER
E) UNBELIEVABLY

WHO IS IN CONTROL IN YOUR RELATIONSHIP?

A) YOU
B) HIM
C) NEITHER
D) BOTH EQUALLY
E) THE KIDS/CAT/DOG

IN THE ARENA OF LOVE WOULD YOU GIVE YOUR MAN:

A) THUMBS UP
B) THUMBS DOWN
C) DIRECTIONS TO THE LIONS
D) MAXIMUS POINTUS
E) ANOTHER GO IN THE RING

COULD YOUR LOVE LIFE DO WITH A BIT OF EXTRA SPICE?

A) NO
B) WHY NOT?
C) ABSOLUTELY
D) ALLERGIC TO SPICE
E) MIND YOUR OWN BUSINESS

Flirtfolio MANagement

Flirting is fundamental to man management. Without it the girl doesn't get the guy and vice versa. When we flirt we are giving out signals, like a peacock flashing its tail. It starts when you first spot your guy, but it doesn't have to stop after you have dated and mated. Flirting is about language, signals and communication – both verbal and non-verbal. You don't stop talking once you are a couple, do you? So keep flirting. It's fun. If you need help getting your flirtfolio together, read on. Digest a statistic first – when you first meet new people, their initial impression of you will be based 55% on your appearance and body language, 38% on the way you speak and only 7% on what you actually say.

You have just arrived at a party. There are some new faces in the room, the atmosphere is lively, you're looking good and feeling confident. Walk tall when you enter the room, looking happy and positive. Swing and roll your hips a little if you are in the mood to flirt. Imagine you are on a catwalk. You are wearing flattering, interesting and colourful clothes, which hug and drape in all the right places (just like you hope you and your man will later). Suddenly, you spot a guy you like the look of. He's in a group but not 'with' anyone. He looks your type and within your feasible romantic orbit. If you have gate-crashed a post-Oscars party and spotted George Clooney, you may want to think twice about your chances. Flirting involves both uncertainty and a risk of rejection, so the best form of communication to employ at first is non-verbal. Body language is the way to start things rolling, because rejection at that stage is less embarrassing. Use the following information with care – you don't want to send out the wrong signals. Start with some eye contact, even from across a crowded room. Hold his gaze for just over a second. If he does the same, he may well be interested. If he looks away and then back again, things could be simmering. If he doesn't, then they probably aren't or he is very short-sighted.

Remember:

F LIRT
L ISTEN
I MITATE
R ESPOND
T EASE

Tips for Flirtfolio MANagement

1. Approach your target, but keep your distance. Once you are about two steps away from him, repeat eye contact. You are now about to leave his social space and enter his personal one (just over an arm's length). If things look positive, step over the border but don't enter his intimate zone (half an arm's length). For this, you need a special invite...

2. If you are standing next to him rather than face-to-face, the intimate zone is a little more relaxed, but if he crosses his arms very firmly and scowls, things are not looking good. If he looks down at the floor, things are looking down too.

3. If things are looking up, give him a few encouraging signals. Look relaxed, approachable, interested. If you are both standing, face him, perhaps with your hands on your hips.

4. Listen attentively to what he is saying. Ask him questions about himself and listen carefully to what he says. Nod in response, be animated and interested.

5. Laugh at his jokes but not like a hyena.

6. Now for a spot of mirroring – echo his movements or posture. He will feel more comfortable and may see you as like-minded, a woman after his own heart (or body).

✔ Do-Do's

These tips could seriously improve your chances of success:

1. Speak and read the language

Watch out for positive responses from your target when flirting. Don't follow the tips slavishly if you are not getting the right vibes. 'Hey, you can't leave yet! I haven't got to the part where I give you a fleeting touch' isn't the way to go (well, he might go but you won't be with him).

Check for positive body-language signals from him, such as increased eye contact, moving closer, open posture, a spot of mirroring, a little touch, gentle verbal teasing. Is he still smiling? Is he looking animated? Is he still there?

2. Slowly does it

If the fleeting touch doesn't get a positive response, you may be moving too fast, so ease up. To him, it may have sounded like the non-verbal equivalent of 'Hi, my name is Lisa – are you single and fertile?' or 'You're a cute guy. Could I have a photo of you for my wedding album?'

It could put some guys off. If he goes quiet or looks anxious, just take your foot off the gas for a while. If he moves closer and looks more interested, you could move up a gear and go for another, less fleeting touch, perhaps on the knee this time.

3. It's all in the tone

What you say and how you say it can be equally important. If your target speaks to you in a slow, sexy, deep drawl with a hint of a question at the end, even when he is making a statement, it's a good sign. So listen out and respond accordingly, not in a depressed

monotone or a childishly excited screech, but with interest in your voice. Don't deliver a monologue, don't interrupt him all the time, don't talk about yourself endlessly (he doesn't know yet just how fascinating you are). Remember, this is a chat, not an interview.

4. Chat up not down

Don't spend too much time worrying about what to talk about. Just be relaxed, flirtatious, light and interesting. If you have a problem on your mind, about work, home or life in general, don't make this the initial or sole topic of conversation for a first

encounter. 'Isn't the world just such a frightening, terrible, dreary, dull place?' won't immediately endear you to him. 'Shall I tell you the story of my rather tragic yet unexciting life?' won't help much. 'Your life sounds so fascinating. Tell me about it...' or 'Great jacket'.

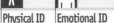
Bedroom MANagement

No, this page is not about more ways to get your guy to keep the bedroom clean. It is about managing your man in bed, livening things up a little and even getting a teensy bit dirty. However, don't feel you have to restrict any of the tips below to those particular four walls – the term 'bedroom' is used loosely. Staying in that specific zone for a while, however, some experts tell us to restrict activity in the bedroom to sleeping, by which they mean banish televisions, DVD players and other unnecessary disruptive elements. All excellent advice to help you get a good night's sleep, but what you need to know about bedroom management has less to do with sleep and more to do with the 'man'.

If you have got as far as the bedroom with your guy, then you probably have the basic principles of flirtation and seduction successfully under your belt (or he has them under his and you succumbed). If you are living together, you are doubtless already rather intimate with your man's behaviour in the sack. But just as a girl can never be too rich, too slim or receive too many boxes of chocolates, she can never have enough hints on how to be a bedroom goddess, revered, honoured and comfortably installed on a pink faux-fur pedestal.

As in other areas of man management, communication plays a fundamental role, together with honesty and openness. If something your guy does in the kitchen or living area annoys you, then you need to talk about it. There's no point keeping it all bottled up inside and becoming increasingly irritated or frustrated, without letting him

know or have the chance to remedy it. The same principle applies in the love department, although you may find the subject requires much more delicate management. Make it a two-way conversation and not a Spanish Inquisition, or he will feel defensive or offended, his manhood under assumed attack. Ask him what he finds most exciting or arousing about you and return the compliments. Later, and more gently, ask if there is anything he doesn't like quite as much about your technique or tactics. Even later and even more gently, and only if the discussion is going well, you could let him know ways in which it could be even more exciting. Don't have this conversation on the bus/at work/at lunch with his parents.

Tips for Bedroom MANagement

1. Ask him to tell you (or write down) a list of the top ten things he loves about your personality and deeds. Do the same about him. Read the lists out to each other. Do this on a quiet evening in on the sofa, but not while watching TV.
2. Then ask him to repeat the exercise, but this time about your body. Ditto for you.
3. Lastly, repeat the exercise once more, but this time your lists should reveal the top ten things you find sexually stimulating about each other.
4. Then ask him if there was one thing he could ask you to do slightly differently in that area what would it be?
5. Use expressions such as 'do differently' or 'even more' or 'even longer' or 'even better/more expertly/more amazingly.'

Keep the signals positive. It's about both of you scoring more out of ten not less.

6. Never ever compare him to one of your 'exes' in a negative way, or he will soon join their ranks. Unless you were planning to dump him anyway...
7. If you don't like the way he kisses/touches/seduces you, don't deflate his ego by saying 'Yuk, that's horrible' or 'Which of your sad exes taught you to do that?' Instead, make it sound like you have come up with an exciting new technique just for him. Say something like 'Let's try it like this for a change' or 'I thought you might like this...' or just show him how you would prefer him to do it without him realising that is what you are doing. Use those feminine wiles.

✔ Do-Do's

The following could seriously improve your love life:

1. Bed and breakfast

The morning after, keep up the surprises and wake him with his favourite breakfast. Bacon and eggs, freshly squeezed juice, a selection of exotic fruits, porridge, muesli, croissants – whatever he would order if you were on holiday. Make him feel special. Bring the papers with the sports pages opened up in readiness. Wear your bikini to serve it if you want to remind him of your recent sun-drenched break, but you may have to compete with last night's scores. Tell him you like surprises, too, especially if they involve travel and luxury hotels…

2. Plan a surprise

Ring your guy at work one Friday and tell him to meet you back at home by a certain time as you have something to show him. Cancel all engagements for Saturday (and maybe Sunday, too). Arrive ahead of him armed with a bottle of champagne, a saucy film, a lap dance kit or nurse's outfit (choose any or all of the above or replace with your own much better suggestions). Set the scene – nice music, delicately scented candles, phones and lights off, sexy outfit on. Send the dog to the movies.

3. Sleep management

If your guy is guilty of one or more of the following three common bedroom crimes – snoring loudly even when not drunk, hogging the mattress every night or grabbing the duvet/quilt/blankets, invest in ear plugs, find natural nasal clearance remedies, buy another duvet or suggest you sleep separately from time to time. Make the latter sound a positive plan not banishment from the kingdom of love. A little absence can make the heart grow fonder and more sleep one night might mean less the next…

4. Stay positive

Tell him how great he is, how really great he is, how much you love him. Before, during and after – he won't mind when. Just keep telling him. Positive reinforcement will boost morale, help keep his pecker up and even improve performance. It will make him feel good. Thank him if he does something kind and considerate, however small. Make him feel appreciated, strong, brainy, brawny, your number one guy. Give him top marks for top form. Underline not undermine. PS. Never let him read this book.

Stress MANagement

Life is stressful – for men and women. It seems to be getting increasingly so as we fill our days with more and more commitments. We are time-poor, activity-rich. There is so much to do and so little time. Huge demands on our time and its limited supply can really stress us out. What is the answer? Try to make time and do less, if possible. It beats making less and doing time, that's for sure. If that makes you smile, stop for a moment to think how much better you feel after a really good laugh? Laughter is an excellent way of de-stressing.

Seriously though, stress is a major factor in our lives today. It is not always a bad thing; good stress can motivate us to achieve more and can be the catalyst for positive change, forcing us to realise that action is needed to deal with the cause of that stress. But too much bad stress can make us ill, physically, emotionally and mentally. All the adrenaline pumping around the system with nowhere to go is not good for the body, and nor are the increases in heartbeat and blood sugar level. Stress, anger and anxiety can make us more prone to heart attacks.

You both get home after a hard day, hackles raised, stressed, preoccupied, tetchy and tired, ready to pounce on the first person you see. You're both snappy and neither of you are shedding crocodile tears – you know the scene. A row develops, you both feel more stressed and the evening is ruined. So what is a girl to do? Managing the stress is the key and here are a few tips on how to do just that:

Breathe Deeply and...

D E D I C A T E   T I M E (for each other)
E A T   W E L L

S L E E P   W E L L
T R E A T   H I M   G E N T L Y
R E W A R D   Y O U R S E L V E S
E X E R C I S E   R E G U L A R L Y
S H A R E   Y O U R   W O R R I E S
S T R E T C H   Y O U R   M I N D

Tips for Stress MANagement

1. Give each other Time Out at the end of a hard day. You can then both debrief and defuse a little, getting rid of any latent anger. Go for a quick walk or do some stretches.
2. Designate one night a week when you do something nice together, such as a visit to the movies, a meal out for just the two of you or a night on the sofa with a DVD and a take-out.
3. Don't take on too many social commitments. Learn to say no from time to time to invitations or requests for favours. Look after yourself and your man – make yourselves Joint Number One for a change. Your friends will understand.
4. Decide together to go easy on tobacco, alcohol, caffeine and snacks, all of which do nothing to relieve stress. Drink herbal teas instead. Try chamomile, passionflower or ginseng.
5. Learn something new to stretch and divert your mind – a foreign language, a new hobby or sport.
6. Buy a punch bag that looks like your boss, his boss or a combination of both and go three rounds with it after work.
7. Go to a funny movie or hire a DVD that makes you enjoy a real belly laugh. Try to think positively and encourage your man to do the same.

✔ Do-Do's

The following could make a big difference to your health and happiness:

1. Share and share alike

Be honest with your partner about your own worries and encourage him to do the same. Encourage him to open up and talk about issues causing him concern or stress, even if it means persuading him gently to admit failure (in his eyes), to say that he is not able to handle, fix or overcome something. Try not to keep worries buried inside – a problem shared is a problem halved after all. If you are really worried about his stress levels, you may want to suggest he sees the GP.

2. Early to bed, early to rise

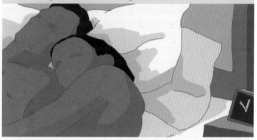

Sleep plays a key factor in keeping stress under control. Both your body and brain need sleep to rest and recuperate, to restore themselves to full capacity. Not sleeping can become a vicious circle in itself. Try to get both of you to bed by a certain time each night (or at least on weeknights) to establish a pattern. Go easy on the alcohol and cigarettes for at least two hours before turning in and finish any exercise at least three hours before bed. Keep the bedroom well ventilated and free of a TV set!

3. Rewards for good behaviour

Try to arrange regular breaks, weekends away or holidays so that you have something to look forward to, budget and schedules permitting. Put some dates in the diary, stick photos of sun-drenched beaches or snow-capped mountains on the refrigerator door to keep you going through the dark days of winter. Make firm bookings and stick to them. Put a wish list on the door, too; when each of you thinks of something you would like to do, write it down and then discuss it. Give yourselves a break (literally).

4. He's number one

After a particularly tough time in your guy's professional or personal life, help him manage the stress in as many ways as you can, given your own concerns and commitments. Make sure he knows that when the tables are turned, he can feel free to return the favours. A nice hot bath, a neck and head massage, a glass of chilled beer ready for when he gets home, a nice meal after a big day. Remind him gently that life is a two-way street and you would like to be Number One when you have your own stresses.

Household MANagement

If you have a man about the house, you might need to persuade him to be more of a man about the house, as it were. If it is the word 'housework' that puts him off, you could refer to it as 'household management' or 'domestic administration', both of which sound more executive and manly. If it is the verbs he doesn't like, you may have more on your plate than you thought. To vacuum, to dust, to wash and to iron (let alone to sweep, wipe, polish, tidy and sort) – all these may turn him off completely. But there are ways to flick that switch and turn him back on.

Let him know how much you would appreciate him helping you do the chores. Do so in a non-confrontational way. Don't make it sound like a nag or you might start the chore wars. Remember, he may not know that you are keen for him to get involved. He may think the house is your private terrain and that trespassers will be prosecuted. Once he is aware that you very much do want him to participate, you might want to make it clear that there is something in it for him. Rewards (or plain bribery) could be in store if he takes out the trash, tidies the bedroom, puts his muddy sports gear in the wash and tries his hand at ironing his own shirts for a change. If he does his share, it will free up time to explore a different set of verbs upstairs. He won't decline to love, to kiss, to cuddle and to frolic.

Draw up a chart of all the household tasks (interior and exterior) and divide the tasks fairly and evenly, bearing in mind practical issues, strong dislikes and schedules. If your guy wants to stick to the jobs related to the car, garden, garage, backyard, exterior walls and roof

If Persuasion Won't Work...

B E D R O O M
R E W A R D S
I N S P I R E
B O Y F R I E N D ' S
E N E R G Y

(including clearing out the gutter), then that may be a good deal. Congratulate him on a job well done – even if you would have done it better, more quickly and thoroughly yourself. Cook his favourite meal, let him be lord of the remote for a whole evening, give him a special massage. It works a treat with dogs so it is in with a chance with your man.

Tips for Household MANagement

1. Tell him that vacuuming is a great way of keeping fit. Research suggests it fights obesity more effectively than jogging, burning around 210 calories per hour. Cleaning and dusting uses about 150 calories per hour.
2. Let him know how sexy you find him when you come home to find he has tidied and cleaned the house and what a god he looks like with a powerful instrument in his hands.
3. Buy the latest model of vacuum with as many knobs, switches and in-built computer programmes as possible. He will love playing with all its buttons.
4. Pin a list of chores and rewards on the door of the refrigerator or on the bedroom wall – he will be motivated to perform.
5. If he makes a bad job of an appointed task, don't give up asking him to do it. It may be a deliberate ploy on his part to avoid a repeat request. Or he could be a real domestic dud.
6. Once the system is working successfully, up the stakes. Tempt him with some seriously big carrots. An entire spring clean and ironing his shirts for a month could result in a weekend with the boys. See if he bites.
7. Make him pay for a cleaner if all else fails...

✔ Do-Do's

Here are just four ways to improve your life immeasurably:

1. Smooth operator

Let him in on five facts about ironing every guy should know. He can burn about 140 calories an hour doing it; he can still listen to his favourite CD while doing it; doing it can (in some men, and who knows he may be one of them?) release feel-good sensations and a great sense of both purpose and achievement; it can make him look like a real smooth operator in your eyes; it will save him money, because if he doesn't do it he will have to take his own shirts to the laundry.

2. Homo houseworkiens

If your man is worried that housework is not for guys, you will have to put him right on that. Inform him of how many males you know who are more than happy to do their share (drop in the names of a few very attractive and single domestic gods to keep him on his toes). Reassure him that none of his friends will tease him, so he can brag about it in the pub. Housework is for men. A man with a dust cloth and broom is just a 21st-century version of one with a loincloth and spear.

3. Cook up a storm

Domestic management is not all about cleaning the house and reacting to mess and dirt. It can be proactive and demand both artistic and scientific skills, particularly in the kitchen. If your man doesn't know one end of a chorizo sausage from another, or the difference between stirring and whipping, suggest you go on a cookery course together. If budget, schedule or existing skills rule this out, do it at home together. Make it fun. Experiment. Make a mess. Have a food fight (but check the rota first).

4. Health and safety

Try explaining that housework is not just about making the place look pretty. Its primary function is to keep the house safe and healthy, to get rid of nasty bugs that lurk in the carpet, the refrigerator, the sofa and, most importantly (for the purposes of this discussion) the bed. Vacuuming the mattress is not about being picky, it's about banning bed bugs who could suck your blood and bring you out in a rash. Make it clear the bed is a no go area if you have to share it with ugly critters with vampire teeth.

Date MANagement

How to Manage Your Man on a Date

There is more to dating than meets the eye, although appearances can sometimes help, hinder, damage or determine the outcome. Here are some hopefully helpful hints on what to wear, say and do at various venues. More importantly a few no-no's may prevent things taking a turn for the worse. It's an interactive affair – just photocopy this page, then cut and paste the elements that make up your perfect date. It's up to you to work out the best route to take, bearing in mind the potential pitfalls.

Venue options

✔ Sample scenario	**✖ Absolute no-no**	**✔ Your perfect date**
Footie match	Work party	affix venue
His favourite team scarf and shirt	Nurse's uniform	affix what (not) to wear
This is really, really exciting	Let's just relax and lie down for a while	affix what (not) to say
To bond	To make an impression	affix gameplan
Wear it, say it and do it - gameplan achieved. You scored!	Don't, don't or you won't – game will be lost. No score!	Now it's up to you to determine where/wear and what? The ball is in your court – put it in the net.

Venue options:
- Rock festival
- Sunday lunch at his parents'
- Romantic walk in the park/ on the beach
- Shopping
- Out for a cappuccino
- Footie match
- Meeting his friends in a bar
- Work party
- Dinner à deux
- Meal at your place

What (not) to wear	What (not) to say		Gameplan
Jimmy Choos	Does my bum look big in this?	Have you thought about what we should call our children?	To bond
Thigh length boots and leathers	Have you heard the scandal about the boss and the woman in accounts?	You are a really dreadful driver!	To move onto the next stage
His favourite team scarf and shirt	Football is even more boring than cricket	Do you shower every day?	To see what sort of father he would make
Doc Martens	I do all his budgets/ coursework for him	Sorry, but I just can't eat this	To find out more about him
Floaty floral dress	Who's the guy in the skirt?	What a noise, let's get out of here now!	To explore a different aspect of his personality
Power suit	I hear you are a very cohesive, effective team	You must be very proud of him	To boost/kickstart his career
Jeans and T-shirt	This is the best food I have had in ages	How cool is that!	To take things to a more intimate level
Dressless strap	This is really, really exciting	I love your aftershave	To make an impression
Nurse's uniform	Let's just relax and lie down for a while	Tell me more!	To motivate him
Fancy dress	You are great behind the wheel	We must do this more often	To find out what he really loves

The Voodoodle

As already mentioned, it is not advisable to play certain games with your man, notably 'Guess what I'm really thinking' or 'No Clue? – doh! Use your male intuition.' It is much better to be straight and direct rather than mysterious and elusive if you are trying to get a message through to the male species. Men don't do mind-reading courses and sadly don't come equipped with crystal balls, although some of the games they play are pretty transparent. However, for those who enjoy a bit of playful fun, here is the game for you. You can play it with your man, but he doesn't need to be present. Ideal scenario...

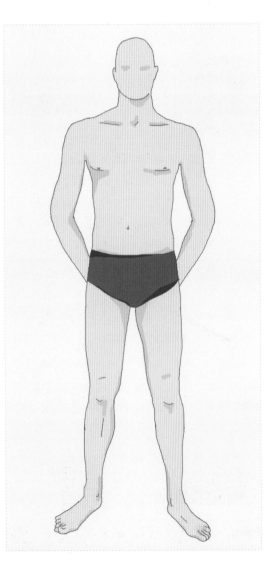

It is called Voodoodle. Qué? Well, it is a slightly different, much more playful version of a Voodoo doll, upon which to take out your frustration or bestow kind rewards, according to how your guy behaves. Photocopy the page and cut out the various elements in the two toolboxes – Prince or Frog – and then apply them to the little cut-out guy. Leave him lying around if you want your own prince or frog to see what fate has befallen him without him even feeling a thing.

No nasty pins needed – they are not really recommended. You can just use a dab of Blutack to put the punishments or rewards in place. Remember, you may want to remove them, so unless he is an ex (or soon to be) and you want to make him a frog forever, don't use glue... Things change in relationships; there are good and bad times. He may be Mr Nasty one day but Mr Nice Guy the next. And if you are really honest, you can be a bit like that too (no need to tell him though). Recent German research has revealed that one of the keys to happy relationships is to give your partner five compliments for each criticism delivered. So one Frog equals five Princes. Sounds like a good deal. They could be on to something...

How to play the game

Your man forgets your birthday. He is rather vain. Spoil his virtual day. Stick a really bad hairstyle on his head and a nasty zit on his lip. Give him Athlete's Foot. He comes home with flowers, chocolate and a huge present. Give a great haircut and a yummy tummy to your Prince Snake-Charming. Let him score a winning goal with his Bootilicious foot. He can score in the virtual and the real world if he is very good. Get the picture? Now get photocopying, cutting and going.

The Prince Box

This box contains the sugar and spice and all things nice you can wish or bestow upon your man. It comes with a small bottle of Passion Potion. Sprinkle a little in the air and things might spice up a little. Let your Prince Charming know how you appreciate everything he has said and done for you recently. Leave the cute cut-out guy lying around and use it to prompt a conversation about how much you appreciate him and love him as a result. Tell him he is on your wish list.

The Frog Box

The contents of this toolbox are much nastier. Snakes and snails and puppy dog tails (well, snakes and worms at least). It also includes a bottle of Toad Tonic, a few drops of which will make things drop off in the love department, so your Frog Prince better watch out. Leave the nasty-looking Voodoodle in the bedroom. He will get the message that he is off the wish list.

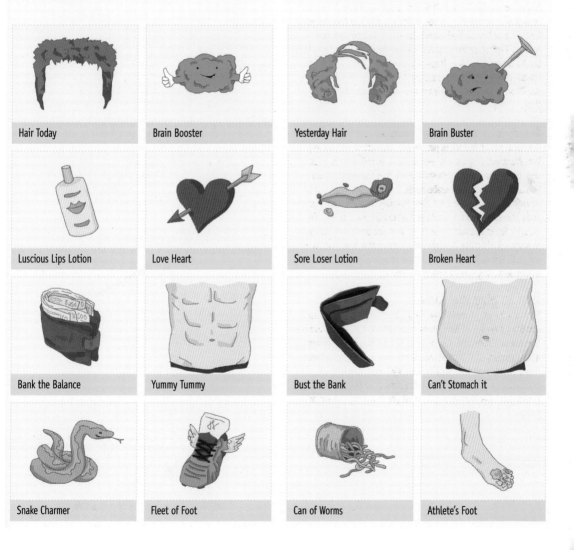

Hair Today	Brain Booster	Yesterday Hair	Brain Buster
Luscious Lips Lotion	Love Heart	Sore Loser Lotion	Broken Heart
Bank the Balance	Yummy Tummy	Bust the Bank	Can't Stomach it
Snake Charmer	Fleet of Foot	Can of Worms	Athlete's Foot

'A SMALL STEP FOR MEN, A GIANT LEAP FOR WOMANKIND' DISHCLOTH DAILY

household management for men

ISBN 1-844-03108-X

'EVERYTHING YOU EVER WANTED TO KNOW BUT WERE AFRAID TO ASK'

vehicle maintenance for women

ISBN 1-84403-258-2

A LITTLE BOOK OF DOMESTIC WISDOM

bathroom

household management for men

ISBN 1-84403274-4

A LITTLE BOOK OF DOMESTIC WISDOM

bedroom

household management for men

ISBN 1-84403273-6

A LITTLE BOOK OF DOMESTIC WISDOM

kitchen

household management for men

ISBN 1-84403272-8

A LITTLE BOOK OF DOMESTIC WISDOM

laundry room

household management for men

ISBN 1-84403271-X